FAMOUS AIRCRAFT OF THE
NATIONAL AIR AND SPACE MUSEUM

Volume 1
EXCALIBUR III
The Story of a P-51 Mustang

Volume 2
THE AERONCA C-2
The Story of the Flying Bathtub

Volume 3
THE P-80 SHOOTING STAR
Evolution of a Jet Fighter

Volume 4
ALBATROS D.Va
German Fighter of World War I

VOLUME **4** FAMOUS AIRCRAFT OF THE NATIONAL AIR AND SPACE MUSEUM

Albatros D.Va
German Fighter of World War I

by Robert C. Mikesh

PUBLISHED FOR THE
National Air and Space Museum
BY THE
Smithsonian Institution Press
WASHINGTON, D.C.
1980

© 1980 by the Smithsonian Institution. All rights reserved
Printed in the United States of America
Reprinted 1988

LIBRARY OF CONGRESS CATALOGING IN PUBLICATION DATA

Mikesh, Robert C.
    Albatros D.Va: German Fighter of World War I
    (Famous aircraft of the National Air and Space Museum; v. 4)
    1. Albatros D. (Fighter planes)   I. National Air and Space
Museum.   II. Title.   III. Series. UG1242.F5M54   358.4′3   80-36711
ISBN 0-87474-633-7

FRONTISPIECE:

This lone Albatros, seemingly on patrol over the Western Front, is actually Cole Palen's superb replica Albatros D.V flying near its home base at Old Rhinebeck Aerodrome in Rhinebeck, New York. (Peter Kilduff)

Cover art by John F. Amendola, Jr.

Unless otherwise noted, photographs are from National Air and Space Museum files, photographed by Dale E. Hrabak, Lawrence Motz, and the author.

Contents

FOREWORD vi

ACKNOWLEDGMENTS vii

I The Airplane 3

II Flying the Albatros 21
    BEFORE STARTING THE ENGINE 22
    STARTING ENGINE 25
    BEFORE TAKE OFF 26
    TAKE OFF 28
    CRUISE 29
    LANDINGS 29

III Restoring the Albatros 31
    FUSELAGE 32
    COCKPIT 44
    ENGINE 48
    WINGS 54
    LOZENGE CAMOUFLAGE FABRIC 68
    EMPENNAGE 76
    FINAL ASSEMBLY 77

IV Other Pertinent Data 87
    CONDENSED WORK-PROGRESS OF THE ALBATROS D.Va 87
    ALBATROS D.Va RESTORATION MAN-HOURS 93
    ALBATROS D.Va SPECIFICATIONS 93
    ALBATROS D.Va PERFORMANCE 94
    MERCEDES D.IIIa ENGINE SPECIFICATIONS 94
    ALBATROS D.V AND D.Va PRODUCTION-BLOCK SERIAL NUMBERS 95
    AIRCRAFT SERVICING 95
    ALBATROS D.Va DRAWINGS 99

Foreword

Although the general public thinks of the air combat in World War I in terms of Fokker D. VIIs and Triplanes, SPADS and Sopwith Camels, the Albatros, in its various models was the most widely used and one of the most important of the German fighter aircraft. Manfred von Richthofen, the legendary "Red Baron," is best remembered as a Triplane pilot, but sixty of his eighty victories came while flying the Albatros.

The story of the Albatros has been often told, but in this record of the beautiful restoration of the National Air and Space Museum's Albatros D.Va, Bob Mikesh has created a unique blend of history, restoration detail, photographs, drawings, pilot comments, and operating instructions. It will appeal equally to the historian, the buff, the model maker, and to those with just casual interest. It is an excellent addition to the Famous Aircraft of the National Air and Space Museum series.

DONALD S. LOPEZ
Chairman
Aeronautics Department

Acknowledgments

Before thanking those that helped in the preparation of this book, recognition must first go to the real "stars" of the project, Garry Cline and Richard Horigan, who spent twenty-six tiring, yet totally dedicated months restoring the Albatros. Their efforts will reflect, for many years to come, the technology for this early period of aviation history in which the Albatros played such an important part. Notes and dimensional sketches outlining the methods by which the work was accomplished were meticulously recorded by Garry, and were valuable assets in the accurate preparation of this book.

An author is privileged when specialists in the subject being presented generously offer their assistance. Heading this list is Peter M. Grosz, a recognized authority on the Albatros and the aircraft of the Central Powers. His guidance and seemingly endless resources on Albatros material has helped the history portion of this book to portray factually the background of the museum's Albatros. Dan Abbott, Peter M. Bowers, Howard G. Fisher, Royal D. Frey, and Peter Kilduff also added valued contributions to this historical section. What began as a mere introduction to the Albatros-type aircraft to preface the section on its restoration, became an in-depth study, based on their contributions.

When former Albatros pilot Paul Strähle of the Federal Republic of Germany agreed to describe the many details of flying this World War I fighter, another chapter was added. His assistance in giving the pilot's perspective of the Albatros was invaluable. Also adding to this chapter was Brig. Gen. Benjamin S. Kelsey (USAF, Retired), with his experiences of flying other aircraft of this vintage, and Cole Palen, who had flown his reproduction of an Albatros at the Old Rhinebeck Aerodrome in New York.

All the engineering aspects of the Albatros were not apparent from the study of the museum's aircraft. Joseph M. DeFiore, David R. McMullen, and Jim Appleby, who have been or are involved in building flyable reproductions of D.Va fighters, made valuable contributions both to the restoration of the Albatros and to this book. Francis P. Garove was often ahead of the restoration project with technical drawings, sketches, and photos that would be needed. Dr. Martin O'Conner provided a sample of the nearly extinct Albatros logo from which to reproduce copies to use for both the restoration and this book. Many years were dedicated by Bob Waugh of South Australia to producing the most accurate drawings of the Albatros that are reproduced here with his kind permission.

There would not have been enough hours in the weeks and months that this study was under preparation, had it not been for Ramona, my understanding wife, who unstintingly gave up her claim on time we would otherwise share together. Without her encouragement and faithful help, this book could not have been completed in its present form.

Others that deserve thanks for their special contributions are Donald S. Lopez, Chairman, Aeronautics Department, NASM; Louise Heskett, Smithsonian Press editor; and designer Gerard A. Valerio all of whom played a vital part in determining how the many words and illustrations are presented to the reader. Also offering invaluable help with this project have been Susan Owen, Dorothy Cochrane, Susan Brown, Robert B. Meyer, and Jay Spenser. To all these and the many that are not mentioned, but had a part in this book, I give my most sincere thanks.

Albatros D.Va

The Albatros D.Va of the National Air and Space Museum was restored to its original colors and markings that are representative of Jagdstaffel 46 to which it may have belonged. The aircraft is exhibited in the World War I Gallery of the museum. (D. Hrabak, NASM)

I

The Airplane

In every prized collection of *things*, there often is at least one "golden nugget" that stands out above all others. Of the aircraft that have been restored in recent years within the National Aeronautical Collection, the Albatros D.Va holds that distinction. Aside from this airplane being recognized as one of the most important fighter planes of World War I, the time, energy, and superior skill that had to be expended in this restoration posed a tremendous challenge. From an almost rotted hulk that had been abused for most of its sixty years of existence, it was restored by craftsmen of the National Air and Space Museum to "like-new" condition—nearly flawless in every detail.

The Albatros factory near Berlin produced the dominant German fighter aircraft of World War I. The first Albatros arrived at the Western Front in August 1916, and subsequent series were important in helping to regain air superiority for the Germans in 1917. In one variant or another, they remained in service with the German air force until the Armistice in November 1918. The Albatros fighters were produced in greater numbers than any other German fighter in that war. The significance of these fighters is further underscored by the fact that nearly all the major German aces scored some or most of their victories with the Albatros as their mount.

Of the D.V. and D.Va series Albatros, there is evidence that 2,505 or more were ordered, yet only one other example of this significant fighter survives, and that one is in the Australian War Memorial Museum in Canberra, Australia. There are no earlier models of Albatros fighters in existence anywhere. No wonder so much pride has been expressed over the restored condition of the Albatros D.Va belonging to the National Air and Space Museum of the Smithsonian Institution in Washington, D.C.

Where did the Smithsonian's airplane come from and what was its story of combat in that war? Always in quest of old and unusual airplanes for what was then known as the National Air Museum, Paul E. Garber, curator of the museum for many years, heard of an Albatros at the DeYoung Memorial Museum in San Francisco. During a trip to California in January 1947, Garber went to the museum and inquired about the airplane, only to be told by a museum attendant that the museum did not own such an airplane.

Disappointed, yet intending to gain something from his visit, Paul Garber took the usual tour through the building. For him this included casually looking behind screens and around storage-room doors left ajar. Behind one of these doors in a storage area was the fuselage of an Albatros resting high upon packing boxes while the wings were hanging on the wall.

Having found what he had hoped for, it was time to speak to the director of the museum. With a disarming apology for having looked somewhere that he should not have, Garber then asked what plans the museum had for the Albatros. The director indicated that this airplane had once been on display, but now the museum specialized in exhibiting art; the plane had already been sold at auction for $500 and was no longer the property of the museum.[1]

---

1. Interview with Paul Garber, and *Cross & Cockade*, Spring 1964, p. 83.

This earliest known photograph of what is now the National Air and Space Museum's Albatros was possibly taken within two years after World War I. The wire mesh over the fuselage gave some protection against birds nesting and unwanted souvenir hunters. The lack of visible tail markings and the serial number may be due to film type or light reflection. (Peter M. Bowers)

The airplane was obviously in poor condition, but Garber knew that he had a rare find. Seeking out the new owner, George K. Whitney, Garber learned that the Albatros was to be staked out on the beach at Playland near Cliff House, San Francisco's famed tourist stop. He asked Whitney if he would donate the airplane to the National Air Museum because of its rarity and historic importance. Whitney agreed to do so on the condition that the museum would pay the cost of packing and transportation.[2] After a lengthy delay until funds became available, Garber made arrangements for it to be moved, assigning the details to the capable hands of Kimbrough S. Brown on the West Coast, a long-time friend of the museum. By August 1949, the airplane had arrived at the museum's temporary storage facility at Orchard Place Airport, Park Ridge, Illinois, now O'Hare International, near Chicago. It remained there until it was moved to the Washington area in 1952, along with the other aircraft of the collection. It was stored at what is now known as the Paul E. Garber Preservation and Restoration Facility in nearby Silver Hill, Maryland. There it stayed in a pathetic state of disrepair until its restoration began in January 1977. The earlier history of this Albatros is very sketchy despite the attempts over the years to reconstruct its backbround.

2. *Cross & Cockade*, Winter 1961, pp. 367-8.

The fully assembled Albatros appeared quite respectable when on exhibit reportedly in California after World War I. All components except tires were present. The lettering "R F" on the nose eroded away over the years and its meaning is unknown. (Clayton Knight Collection, via F. Garove)

A left-side view of the Albatros at the same exhibit location. The sign at the nose merely identifies this as a "Captured German Airplane." (Clayton Knight Collection, via F. Garove)

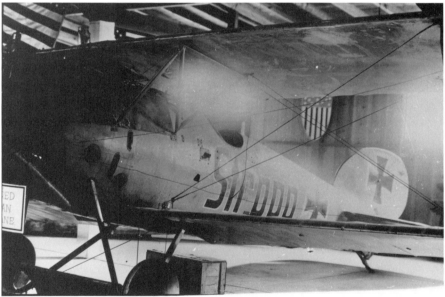

The earliest known record is of its presentation to the DeYoung Memorial Museum on July 13, 1919, by Congressman Julius Kahn.[3] How it came into his possession has not been determined, but the identification label at the time credited it as a gift from the French government.[4]

Sometime during the mid-1930s, aviation historian Peter M. Bowers recalls that the Works Project Administration (WPA) did a makeshift restoration on the airplane. A basketball-size hole in the bottom of the airplane was patched, the bottom of the upper wing was painted gray, and overly thick wooden struts with half the normal number of bracing wires managed to hold the airplane together; also, the right aileron was missing. It was recognizable

3. *Cross & Cockade*, Summer 1971, p. 190.
4. *Cross & Cockade*, Summer 1963, pp. 195-7.

This 1937 picture of the Albatros in the "War Room" of the DeYoung Memorial Museum in San Francisco shows that the rudder, right aileron, and cowling were already missing. The wheel axle is merely tied below the struts, and tires have been added. (F. McIntosh via Cross & Cockade*)*

even then that this airplane was made up from parts of several Albatros fighters; there was a mix of lozenge and painted camouflage along with the early style Iron Cross or *Eisernes Kreuz* on the fuselage and tail, and the late style straight-sided cross or *Balken Kreuz* on the lower wings.[5]

Sometime before the airplane left the DeYoung Museum, perhaps in the 1930s, the rudder was broken off, leaving only the front structural bar which was held to the fin by its hinges.

Over the years, one of the stories surrounding this Albatros was that it was once flown by German pilot Leutnant J. Willie Mauss.[6] The statements made by Mauss that were carried in the *Berkeley Gazette* of October 30, 1931, will not support careful scrutiny. They were made at a time when no one could come forth to question his claims, and he achieved some measure of fame based on his own imagination and statements. There is no record of a Ltn. J. Willie Mauss having been a German pilot in World War I, and therefore these fradulent statements need not be perpetuated here.

What then is the true service history of the airplane? We can arrive at some interesting conclusions based partially on fact and partially on circumstantial evidence. There are several solid clues that give the historian a fairly substantial picture. These are the airplane's serial number, cross styles, battle damage, personal markings, and tail markings.

During restoration, the aircraft's military serial number D.7161/17 was discovered under several coats of paint on the fin. The serial number belongs

5. Ibid.
6. *Cross & Cockade,* Spring 1971, p. 90.

The only other surviving Albatros D.Va is at the Australian War Memorial Museum in Canberra. This Albatros, serial D.5390/17, is now restored, but this photo was taken shortly after it was brought down by an R.E.8 of No. 5 Squadron, Australia Flying Corps.

to a batch of 550 Albatros D.Va fighters ordered in October 1917, the last batch that the Albatros factory near Berlin produced during the war.[7] While definitive German production records relating to World War I were destroyed during World War II, recent research indicates that production of the Albatros fighter series ended in April 1918. This was determined by working backward from known monthly Albatros D.Va production figures of 120, 174, and 170 aircraft in April, March, and February 1918. This conclusion assumes that aircraft were built sequentially, which, while logical, may not have always been the case.

The aircraft identification insignia crosses provide a clue to the end of its operational service. On March 17, 1918, *Idflieg* (Inspectorate of Flying Troops) issued Order No. 41390 stating that all German aircraft were to change the *Eisernes Kreuz* (Iron Cross) to the *Balken Kreuz* (straight cross) as soon as possible but no later than April 15, 1918. The reason for the change was because pilots near the threshold of perception tended to confuse the Iron Cross insignia at a distance for a cockade.

7. Peter M. Grosz, "The Agile and Aggressive Albatros," *Air Enthusiast Quarterly*, No. 1, 1976.

One of the restorers of the National Air and Space Museum's Albatros illustrates, with a rod, the path of the bullet that caused battle damage to this airplane. The bullet passed through the right machine-gun mount, then penetrated the emergency fuel tank, as pointed out by Richard Horigan, then lodged in the right magneto. This damage alone was not severe enough to have brought the Albatros down.

Before restoration, the museum's Albatros had Iron Crosses on its sides and fin, and straight crosses on the lower wings. This would indicate that it was put out of action between March 17, 1918, and April 15, 1918. Two other observations are apparent. First, the wings appear to have come from different airplanes as the quality of their construction indicates different workmanship. Second, the possibility exists that this airplane was assembled from parts by the Allies and very likely this may have happened after its arrival in the United States.

Battle damage to this airplane is perhaps the most interesting clue upon which to speculate about its last flight. A bullet, supposedly from an Allied aircraft, passed over the pilot's right ear, entered the front right machine-gun mount, penetrated the front corner of the emergency fuel tank and stopped when it struck the right magneto. Contrary to earlier speculation, this single round did not necessarily force this airplane down, provided everything else was working properly during this flight. A safe landing could have been made if the other magneto continued to operate properly. Since the emergency fuel tank could not be pressurized for fuel flow, the remainder of the flight would have to be continued with the main tank which may well have contained enough fuel to allow a safe landing. Any number of things could have gone wrong which when amplified by either of these two limitations caused by battle damage may have brought the airplane down in an emergency situation, possibly into Allied hands. One more assumption that can be made is that the airplane never flew again as the fuel tank had not been repaired or replaced, and the missing magneto implies that the damaged one was removed and never replaced.

Additional evidence of the service history of the airplane, and even today the most tantalizing mystery, is the name "Stropp" painted on the sides. This according to German marking practice, is the personal marking of the pilot. It was hoped that that name would be found on a list of German pilots who fought in World War I. German lists checked so far have revealed no such name. This is not easily recognized by Germans as a common German family name, nor is it the name of a German town.

Following the family-name possibility one step further, however, Garry Cline, one of the restorers of the Albatros, checked the Washington/Maryland suburban telephone directory and wrote to the only Stropp listed for a possible answer. Michelle Stropp replied that the name was very rare and could be possibly a short form of Stroppa. Her grandfather brought the name from Finland; however, it originated in Turkey many generations prior to that.

Thinking that the Musee de l'Air in Paris might have some record of the airplane, and the name—since the airplane allegedly came from France—a check was made with its staff, but they had no knowledge of the transaction.

The most plausible explanations have been submitted by various native-born Germans; one being that "Stropp" is a nautical German word meaning *strop* or *sling*. Another suggests that if the pilot was familiar with the dialect around the Cologne area, it can be interpreted as being a capricious or mischievous boy who is always up to no good, yet is never really bad. Its purpose for being painted on this Albatros, whether it be the name or nickname of the pilot, airplane, or whatever, remains unsolved. Should the answer ever be known, the many dead-end paths that have been taken will undoubtedly bear little relation to the intended usage of the word. A bold marking such as this for the museum's Albatros is very representative of the personalized markings that seemed the rule rather than the exception for German aircraft.

There has been considerable speculation over the years as to the tail markings found on this Albatros. The question was whether these personalized markings were for the pilot, or were these the markings for a *Jagdstaffel* (generally referred to as *Jasta*—fighter unit). Since there is no complete description of all the *Jasta* markings that were used in World War I, the thought-to-be black and yellow tail stripes remained unidentified. And too, there is a very remote possibility that these tail colors were painted on the aircraft after it was brought to the United States. The earliest known photo of this airplane implies a blank fin, but this could be due to a reflection since the aircraft number is not visible in this picture either, yet it is known to have been in place from the time of its manufacture. Only in recent years, after the paint had eroded sufficiently, could the aircraft number D.7161/17 be detected from under the coats of paint on the fin.

Be that as it may, one mystery about the tail color and markings was resolved during this restoration. For years, the tail stripes were thought to be black and yellow, but as the tail was being disassembled, protected areas showed that, under the crust, the "dark-stripe" color was actually a dark olive green. If these were the true markings for this Albatros while it was operational, and there is no reason to believe otherwise, something can be said of its wartime service.

When Howard G. Fisher and Dan Abbott, students of World War I aviation history, learned of the true tail-stripe colors, they quickly and jubilantly recognized this unit marking as belonging to *Jasta* 46. Their research into the operational history of this unit weaves an interesting background that relates to the museum's Albatros. They found that *Jagdstaffel* 46 was formed at Graudenz on December 17, 1917, as part of Germany's *Amerika Program*. The program's objective was to build up German strength as rapidly as possible for a decisive blow in the West before American equipment and manpower became an overwhelming factor against Germany. Under the program, German fighter units were to be increased from 40 to 80.

From January through March 20, 1918, *Jasta* 46, based at Ascq, was part of *Jagdruppe Nord* of the Sixth Germany Army. This group consisted of *Jastas* 18, 46, and 57, and was commanded by Oblt. Rudolf Berthold, a famous German ace. On March 20, 1917, *Jasta* 46 was based at Beviflers, seven miles southeast of Cambrai, and was attached to *Jagdruppe* 2. *Jasta* 5, the other fighter unit attached to *Jagdruppe* 2, commanded by Oblt. Richard Flashar, was stationed a few miles away at Neuvilly. On April 17, 1918, the two *Jastas* moved forward to Lieramont where they remained for one month before being transferred to Cappy on May 18, 1918. In July, *Jasta* 37 was added to *Jagdruppe* 2. The unit was moved to Moislains on July 18, 1918. The final transfer of *Jasta* 46 was to Villers sur Nicole in October where it remained until the end of the war.

During its existence, *Jasta* 46 was commanded by three officers: Ltn. Rudolf Matthaie was leader from the beginning until his death practicing dogfighting with one of his pilots on April 17, 1918. Command then passed to Oblt. Josef Loeser who was killed in action on June 3, 1918. Ltn. Otto Creutzmann assumed command until the Armistice.

Jasta 46 had a distinguished and honorable service record. During its entire life it fought against the best squadrons that the Royal Flying Corps, later the Royal Air Force, could offer. It was credited with at least 45 confirmed victories and probably many more since the records are incomplete. Its highest scoring aces included Ltn. Oskar Hennrich (18 victories), Offstv. Robert Heibert (13 victories), Ltn. Rudolf Matthaei (10 victories), Ltn. Otto Creutzmann (7 victories), and Ltn. Helmut Steinbrecher (5 victories).

While on the Western Front, *Jasta* 46 used several types of aircraft, often at the same time. Originally the equipment consisted of Albatros D.III fighters. In February 1918, *Jasta* 46 began receiving Albatros D.V and Pfalz D.III fighters. In the spring of 1918, *Jasta* 46 received Albatros D.Va fighters. And finally, it is believed that *Jasta* 46 had been equipped with Fokker D.VII fighters which they flew until the end of the war.

The identification markings of *Jasta* 46 consisted of yellow and green stripes on all of the tail section except for the rudder which was white. Photographs indicate that the stripping was similar in width and angle on all types of aircraft used, but there were apparently some minor variations with respect to the white applied to the rudder and occasionally the fin. The National Air and Space Museum's aircraft style and coloration could be considered standard.

Jasta 46 did not change the wing camouflage pattern as applied at the factory. The Albatros wing camouflage came in two types: the early D.Va pattern consisted of green and mauve sections, and the later pattern consisted of a five-color lozenge pattern on a preprinted fabric. It is the later style that is seen on the museum aircraft's wings. Fuselages were left in their factory-varnished, natural wood color finish as is the case of the museum's Albatros. Metal fittings were factory painted, usually gray or green. *Jasta* 46 aircraft had a personal marking on their fuselage sides. Some for this unit that have been identified are a shooting star, a lightning bolt, black-and-white

First in the line of single-seat Albatros fighters was the D.I of 1916. With the exception of the wings, lines of all Albatros fighters remained quite similar.

bands, the letter "P," white chevrons, and of course, one aircraft with the word "Stropp."

The period March 21 to April 15, 1918, is of particular interest to historians concerned with the "Stropp" Albatros. It is reasonable to assume that Albatros D.7161/17 did not have an operational life past the latter date because the Iron Crosses on its fuselage and fin would have been changed per *Idflieg* Order No. 41390. This period is also significant because it coincides with the German spring offensive of 1918 which consisted of some of the heaviest air fighting of the war. *Jasta* 46 during this time was stationed at the exact center of the German thrust to throw a wedge between the British and French armies. Losses during this campaign were unusually high; for example, during three days, March 22, 23, and 24, the British claimed 112 German planes shot down in the sector patrolled by *Jasta* 46 and other German squadrons.[8] German claims were equally high. On both sides, because of the swift German advances, administrative and organizational chaos was rampant. The situation was so confused that for several days the German High Command was unable to issue daily operation orders to its aircraft fighter units. Fuel, supplies, and replacement parts were critically short.[9] British daily squadron records for this period are often missing, and this may be one factor to help explain why no record of the capture of Albatros D.7161/17 has been found.

As stated earlier, what is known of the museum's Albatros is partially fact and partially circumstantial evidence. History has taught researchers to be

---

8. Jones, H.A., *The War in the Air*, vol. IV (Oxford: Clarendon Press, 1934), pp. 301-317.
9. Ibid.

There was little apparent change between the first two models of the Albatros. The D.II above shows the cabane strut modified from a pylon to an "N" arrangement, affording better visibility for the pilot. (Smithsonian Institution, Shell Companies Foundation, Inc., Collection)

The clean lines of the bullet-shaped Albatros fuselage are even more apparent on the D.III. Wing tips took on a more rakish design of this model. (Smithsonian Institution, Shell Companies Foundation, Inc., Collection)

Dubbed the "V-strutter" by Allies, the Albatros D.III copied the narrow lower wing and V-strut arrangement from the French Nieuport. This Albatros D.III is from the 2 Marine Feld Jagdstaffel flying over Flanders, during the summer in 1917. (Smithsonian Institution, Shell Companies Foundation, Inc., Collection)

This frame from a World War I motion-picture film shows a woodworker at the Albatros Works finishing an Albatros D.III rear fuselage former with top and bottom fin stiffeners. Although standard patterns were used throughout the construction, most of the fabrication was done by hand.

prepared for the unexpected and the unusual. What is known is that the museum has a treasured possession, an aircraft of a type that is very rare, historically very significant, and most representative of its gender. It is one of very few aircraft in the collection that has seen combat.

The production of Albatros fighters began with the D.I in 1916. From the very beginning, these fighters were revolutionary in design and appearance. Their semi-monocoque, smoothly contoured plywood fuselage was a radical change from the boxy, fabric-covered structures then in general use. The D.I was the brainchild of Dipl. Ing. Robert Thelen, then the chief engineer at the Albatros-Gesellschaft für Flugzeug-unternehmungen m.b.H. at Johannisthal, near Berlin, assisted by two other engineers, Dipl.Ing. Schubert and Ing. Gnaedig. The D.II that followed was nearly identical to the D.I except for a slight difference in wingspan and area, and a modified cabane-strut arrangement. These 160 hp Mercedes-powered single-seat fighters entered German fighter units in the autumn of 1916 at a time when the Fokker monoplanes had lost supremacy to Allied fighters. When the faster and more heavily armed Albatros fighters attacked the British D.H.2 pusher fighters, which had been built to counter the Fokker monoplane, the de Havillands were often helpless and could only elude their attackers if the pilot had superior flying ability.

In the fall of 1916 a new Albatros fighter was tested; the D.III. The aircraft was so superior to the others under consideration that Albatros was awarded the largest single production contract of any German fighters up to that time. The new airplane, a modified D.II, featured a narrow-chord lower wing adapted from the French sesquiplane Nieuport Scouts that had impressed German pilots with its agile maneuverability. The pilots' field of vision was greatly improved due to the smaller chord lower wing. An airfoil-shaped Teves and Braun radiator was centrally placed in the top wing. Pilots soon asked that the radiator be offset so that the connecting water pipes would not hinder the pilot's field of vision, especially gun-aiming. The radiator was placed on the starboard side of the center section. Some sources claim the

Many hands make light work at setting the top wing of this Albatros D.III in place on the cabane struts at the Albatros factory. The D.III remained in production alongside the new D.V for several months.

reason for the offset was that, should the radiator be punctured, it would release a stream of scalding water in the pilot's face. Although this was not the instigating reason for the change, it would seem to have some merit. On the other hand, all Austro-Hungarian D.III fighters of which 454 were built, retained the center-line wing radiators.

The new Albatros D.III met with immediate acceptance. The average pilot found it an easy airplane to fly, without bad traits; above all, it was an effective combat machine. It did, however, have an initial shortcoming in the form of recurrent lower wing failure that normally occurred during prolonged dives. It is believed that the center of pressure on the single-spar lower wing moved forward, causing flutter and then wing failure as the flutter amplitude exceeded design strength. During extensive testing, the structural strength of the wings proved to be more than adequate under static-load tests. The problem was eased to an acceptable degree by reinforcing the wing structure and by improving manufacturing quality control.

The D.IV, of which three were ordered and presumably only one was built, was conceived only for investigating the operating characteristics of a geared 160-hp Mercedes engine. Soon to follow in the progression of Albatros fight-

Not all landings ended happily on the often rough, unprepared airfields. The green-tailed Albatros D.V of Oblt. Flashar, Jasta 5, has a "mailed gauntlet" painted across its fuselage. The aileron linkage method is the only prominent feature that distinguishes a D.V from a D.Va. (Puglisi)

Two MG 08/15 machine guns were mounted above the engine in front of the pilot. Should they jam in combat, they could be reached and cleared by the pilot. Shown here is Ltn. Hans Hamscher of Jagdstaffel 37. (Neal W. O'Connor, via Garove)

ers was the D.V whose prototype was completed in early 1917. It was designed to be a lighter airplane than the D.III. It had a redesigned fuselage which dispensed with the flat sides of the earlier fighters and introduced a truly elliptical contoured fuselage. The wings were similar to the D.III, but the aileron control cables were located in the top wing rather than running through the lower wing.

The horizontal tail and vertical fin remained unchanged from the D.III, but the rudder was redesigned with a more rounded outline. The lower tail fin on which the tail skid was mounted was modified and is a handy identification feature. In all, the new airframe was reduced in empty weight from the D.III by about 70 pounds, primarily due to changes in fuselage construction. The headrest, a feature of early production machines was usually removed by

The major external feature that distinguished this Albatros D.Va from the D.V is the visible aileron control cables leading from the lower wing to the top wing mounted aileron. The small strut from the leading edge to the V-strut was retrofit to D.V and early production D.Va fighters and later incorporated into production craft. (Puglisi)

pilots, as this tended to restrict vision to the rear. Although both the D.III and the D.V were powered by the 160-hp Mercedes engine, the D.V by being lighter, was the better performing aircraft. Later, the engine compression ratio was raised and eventually oversized cylinders and pistons were fitted that up-rated the power to 185 hp at higher altitudes.

The manufacture of the D.III did not end with the appearance of the D.V. In fact, additional orders were placed for this very good airplane and both were produced simultaneously until early 1918.

Armament consisted of two fixed 7.92-mm machine guns, officially known as *Maschinengewehr* MG 08/15,[10] protruding through the upper fuselage decking in front of the pilot. These were synchronized to fire through the propeller arc by a direct cable-drive interrupter gear. The guns were fired by twin thumb-buttons on the control column actuated through a Bowden cable.

10. This gun is unofficially known under various names, i.e., Maxim 08/15 and Spandau 08/15 by the Allies, and simply MG 08/15 in German usage. It was built by the Royal Gun Factory in Spandau, and was based on the machine-gun design by Hiram S. Maxim.

They could be operated independently by either thumb, or simultaneously with one thumb placed on a common recess across both buttons.

The initial exuberance over the new D.V machines was quickly dampened after a rash of upper wing-spar failures occurred just outboard of the wing-strut attachment fitting. Again, the reason was not fully understood as the structural strength of the wings proved to be more than adequate under the static load test. The engineers at *Idflieg* cannot be faulted, for the state of fatigue, torsion, vibration, and flutter-failure analysis was still in its infancy. But even at this early period of designing aircraft structures, the Germans were already exploring active vibration testing of full-size airframes, certainly at a more advanced level than American, French, or British testing.

The remedy to the problem appeared in the Albatros D.Va whose delivery began in the late autumn of 1917. Added strength was in the form of heavier wing ribs, stronger wing spars, and additional fuselage members. A small brace from the lower part of the wing V-strut to the wing leading edge was erroneously thought by many as a differentiating mark of the D.Va. The brace was retrofitted on D.V and D.Va fighters as an additional safety feature to increase the rigidity of the lower wing.

Aileron operation on the D.Va reverted to the system used on the D.III whereby the cables were led through the lower wing and ran vertically near the wing strut to the aileron actuating arms. This is the only external structural feature that easily distinguishes the D.V from the D.Va. In fact, it has been noted that the D.Va top wing is identical in shape and size to that of the D.III; differing by having a shorter length aileron actuating arm and heavier construction material.

Airframe strengthening of the D.Va, unfortunately increased its overall weight nearly 50 pounds *above* that of the earlier D.III which in turn negated the intent of the newer model and resulted in a performance drop. The D.Va remained in production until April 1918, which was several months past the production phase-out of the D.III.

Production of the Albatros machines ended at a time when a better fighter was introduced, namely the Fokker D.VII and Pfalz D.XII. Both the parent Albatros factory at Johannisthal, a suburb of Berlin, and its subsidiary, the Ostdeutsche Albatros Werke (OAW) at Schneidemühl switched production to the Fokker D.VII beginning in March 1918.

Despite the earlier shortcomings of the Albatros fighters—which have been overemphasized by aviation historians when compared to the problems experienced by other aircraft—approximately 4,800 Albatros fighters of all types were produced during the conflict. So completely did the Albatros airplanes monopolize German fighter production that not only were they in overwhelming use throughout 1917, but as late as April 30, 1918, when the Pfalz D.IIIa, Fokker Triplane, and miscellaneous fighters were in use. Of the total German fighters at the front 1,233 or 58 percent were Albatros D.III, D.V, and D.Va. Nearly every German *Jagdstaffel* had within their inventory one or more types of Albatros single-seat fighters. These remained in action in considerable numbers to the end of hostilities.

Many notable airmen flew D.V and D.Va pursuits. Among these were Ltn. Hermann Goering, who later was to head Hitler's *Luftwaffe* in World War II. Albatros fighters of *Jasta* 21 led by the Bavarian ace Hptm. Eduard Udet (62 victories), Hptm. Adolf von Tutschek (27 victories), and Obltn. Erich Loewenhardt (53 victories). Manfred von Richthofen scored most of his 80 victories in the Albatros—and not the Fokker Triplane as legend implies. During an air duel in a D.V, von Richthofen, the "Red Baron," was seriously wounded, yet was able to nurse his crippled airplane to a safe landing before

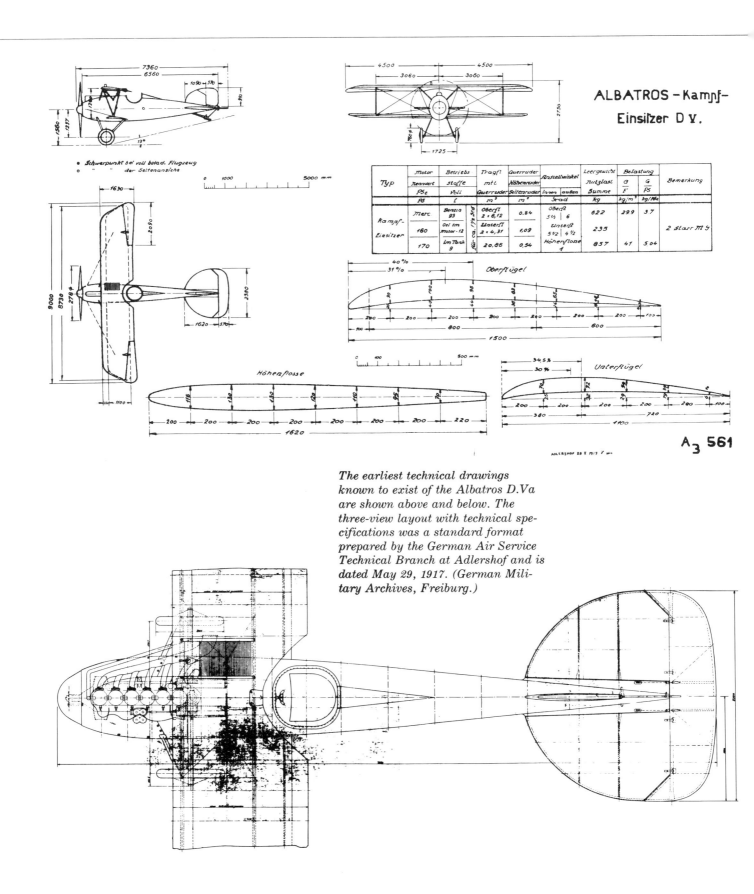

The earliest technical drawings known to exist of the Albatros D.Va are shown above and below. The three-view layout with technical specifications was a standard format prepared by the German Air Service Technical Branch at Adlershof and is dated May 29, 1917. (German Military Archives, Freiburg.)

A long service life for this Albatros D.Va is indicated by its 1917 serial number and the narrow Balken-Kreuz insignia design introduced in the autumn of 1918. This Albatros was flown by Jasta 59, at Hornaing, Belgium, in September 1918. (via Hanns-Gerd Babe/Kilduff)

collapsing. Undaunted, he later flew another Albatros to lead his unit during the Battle of Cambrai.

The Albatros was able to give a lively account of itself, especially in the hands of skilled pilots. "As a matter of fact" states Peter M. Grosz, a recognized historian and authority on German World War I aircraft, "it was an excellent-handling aircraft even in the hands of a mediocre pilot and that is one reason it remained at the Front so long." During the course of Mr. Grosz's assistance with providing many facets of the Albatros D.Va history, he had the following remark to make which summarizes quite well the status that the Albatros commands in aviation history.

The Albatros D.V. was better than any other German fighter when it was placed in production. If a better fighter had been designed by Pfalz, Roland, Fokker, LVG, etc., then it would have been ordered and built in quantity. Although politics may have played some part in the matter [but far less than often implied], the choice of fighters, bombers and two-seaters was a very sophisticated process, based on many hours of careful testing. If the Albatros D.Va had any shortcomings, it was due to the fact that it remained at the Front too long and was then surpassed by newer and superior British aircraft. Perhaps the Fokker D.VII with its 180-hp Mercedes was not that much better than the Albatros D.Va. The Fokker D.VII did not win its handsome reputation until the advent of the BMW.IIIa 'high-altitude' engine.

II

Flying the Albatros

"The Albatros D.Va was a magnificent fighter plane, and inasmuch as its performance is concerned, it was equal to the Fokker D.VII."

This summation of the flying qualities of the Albatros came from Paul Strähle of the Federal Republic of Germany in response to my many questions about flying this early airplane. During World War I, Mr. Strähle was a German Air Force pilot, assigned to *Jastas* 18 and 57. He had flown all types of German fighters of that period including the Albatros. In combat he achieved fourteen victories. An active pilot for sixty-five years at the time of my inquiries, Mr. Strähle's firsthand experiences have been of great value in helping to record the operating procedures and flying qualities of the Albatros.

World War I aircraft were relatively simple to operate and therefore there was very little written instruction for pilots on their operation. Pilots' checklists and flight manuals for specific airplanes did not come into recognized usage until shortly before World War II. With the passing of time, however, many of the operating principles of these early flight systems have been drastically changed. With few written instructions, it sometimes is difficult to understand their operation. In an effort to create such a record, information from a number of sources has been consolidated into a format like that used today in flight handbooks for modern aircraft. This information is based largely upon Mr. Strähle's experience in flying the Albatros, along with the notes made by Cole Palen from his recent flight operation of a reproduction Albatros which he bases at Old Rhinebeck Aerodrome, New York. Dave McMullen, who is building an Albatros for himself, provided an English translation from a Daimler instruction manual which describes the operating procedures for the Mercedes DIII and DIIIa engines. Other operating details have been formulated following a study of the systems installed in the museum's Albatros. Added to this was the knowledgeability of Joseph M. DeFiore, whose considerable experience with Mercedes aircraft engines both as a restorer and builder of vintage aircraft proved most helpful. This writer's own flying experience over the years, which admittedly has been in far more modern equipment than the Albatros, also played a part.

After any enemy engagement, those on the ground were always eager to be on hand to hear of these aerial duals. The Albatros gave a good account of itself in the hands of an experienced pilot, such as Rittmeister Manfred von Richthofen (in center, facing camera). (Peter M. Bowers)

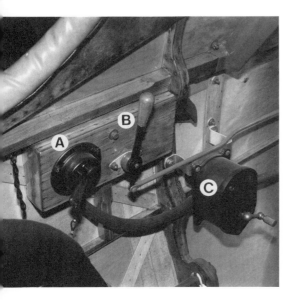

The left side of the cockpit contains the spark-control handle, often misidentified by viewers as the throttle which is actually on the left control stick handle.

The cockpit of the Albatros D.Va looks sparse since it has no instrument panel. Forward of the cartridge belt container (F) are the two ammunition cans, side by side. Guns were fired separately or simultaneously by thumb recessed buttons in the center between control grip handles.

At first glance into the cockpit of the Albatros, it is apparent that there are few instruments, and for that matter, no instrument panel at all. What is equally as interesting is the number of strange valve handles and screw knobs that have not been seen in aircraft for many years. To learn how all these items work, let us take an imaginary familiarization flight in the Albatros.

According to Mr. Strähle, there was little or no preflight walk-around made by the pilot to check the airframe and engine as is expected today. This was entrusted to the mechanic or crew chief. However, most pilots did give a tug or two on the wires for reassurance that everything was held together properly.

The Daimler Engine Operation Manual lists the following items to be checked by the mechanic before flight.

1. The propeller is properly seated on the hub, bolts are tight and safetied.
2. Bolts are secure that hold engine cylinders.
3. Engine mount bolts are taut and safetied.
4. Magnetos tightly secured.
5. Ignition cable connections secure.
6. Rocker arms and rocker rollers move freely.
7. The gap for inlet and exhaust tappets is checked with a feeler gauge. Clearance for inlet tappet is 0.432 mm and exhaust tappet is 0.355 mm.
8. All airframe bracing wires are taut.
9. Turnbuckles are safetied.
10. Flight controls move freely with no slack in control linkages.

With the outside check completed, we are ready to enter the cockpit. Getting into the Albatros was rather difficult compared to other aircraft. Placing the right foot into the recessed step on the lower fuselage got one off the ground, but it was a very long reach to get the left foot over the cockpit coaming and onto the seat. The use of an ordinary stepladder was the method most often preferred, especially when wearing heavy winter clothing which sometimes included a long leather coat.

BEFORE STARTING THE ENGINE

The Albatros seat is quite comfortable and similar to a leather upholstered chair with armrest-high sides. What is most puzzling is that the seatbelt is secured outside these sides and when fastened across the lap, it does not hold the pilot securely in the seat but merely keeps him from falling out of the plane. The shoulder straps can be snugly fitted and therefore may offer the restraint needed.

Seat adjustment is fore and aft only. A position locking thumbscrew is located on the lower left side of the seat.

A visual cockpit check prior to engine start for the Albatros can be accomplished in approximately fifteen seconds by an experienced pilot. For a better understanding of all these cockpit gadgets however, let us run through the checklist starting from the left and continuing clockwise. (Letters in parentheses refer to those items similarly marked in the cockpit photographs.)

(1) Magneto Switch Key (A)—Insert into socket and check to be OFF. (When aircraft is unattended, key is removed from socket and hangs free on chain. This renders the ignition system safe from accidentally starting the engine should the propeller be turned.

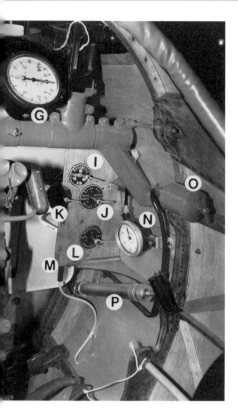

An unusual control lock was the sleeve around the control column that is connected by a yoke to the walking beam for the control column. This sleeve freely moves up and down as the control is moved fore and aft until locked by the pilot by turning the hand-locking screw under the left-hand grip.

NOTE

The switch handle can be turned to four different positions. In position O the two engine-driven magnetos and the starting magneto are OFF. In position marked M1 (for start) the left magneto and the starting magneto are turned ON. In position M2, the magneto on the right side and the starting magneto are on while the left magneto is off. In position 2, both engine-drive magnetos and the starting magneto are ON.

(2) Spark Control Handle (B)—Fully retarded.

(3) Starting Magneto (C)—Check. Do not crank. (Crank can be removed for safety purposes.)

(4) Auxiliary Throttle Handle (D)—In the stowed position. While holding this handle with the left hand, move the control stick throttle (E) through its complete travel to ensure that the two are not connected.

NOTE

In the event that throttle linkage is severed to the throttle handle on the control stick, push auxiliary throttle handle all the way forward to the stop. A detent in the end of the rod will lock to the throttle control at the carburetor and normal operation can be resumed through this auxiliary throttle-linkage handle.

(5) Cartridge Belt Container (F)—In place and secure. (This is removed after each flight during which the guns have been fired, emptied of the used cartridge belt, and replaced on the rear side of ammo box in front of pilot.)

(6) Tachometer (G)—At rest on "Zero." (Presumably this is set at an angle so that during normal operations this needle points vertically for ease in reading at a glance. This practice of rotating the orientation of instruments followed in later years until instrument designers took this into consideration.)

(7) Fuel pressure Gauge (H)—Resting at "Zero." (Should read 0.25 atmospheric pressure while engine is operating.)

(8) Fuel Pressure Gauge Valve Control (I)—ON. (Turn valve OFF if gauge causes an air pressure leak.)

(9) Air Pump Selector Valve (J)—BOTH. (In the event there is a failure in one of these air pressure sources, set selector to the operational source only.)

(10) Fuel Tank Air Pressure Valve (K)—MAIN TANK.

(11) Fuel Tank Flow Selector Valve (L)—PRESSURIZED FUEL.

NOTE

With air pressure selector handle (K) turned to EMERGENCY TANK, fuel from the Emergency Fuel Tank can be used in two ways: (1) With handle (L) set to the left—NOTB. (Emergency Fuel) fuel flow is from the Emergency Tank to the carburetor through the fuel-air control unit. (2) With the handle (L) up—NOTBENZ. FULLEN (Emergency Fuel Filling) fuel flow is the same as (1) above, but also flows into main tank at the same time so that the Emergency Tank can be emptied into the Main Tank and total fuel quantity can be read from fuel gauge that measures the Main Tank only.

NOTE

For normal engine start and flight, all cockpit valve handles point down.

(12) Open drain cock (M) on fuel filter and release a small quantity of fuel before closing. (Valve is located below and behind fuel panel.)

(13) Fuel Quantity Gauge (N)—Check quantity. (Main Tank reading only, which holds 80 liters.)

(14) Water Pump Greaser (O)—Apply a slight twist to assure pressure is

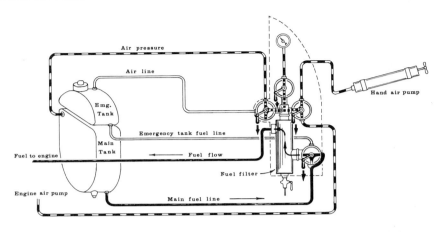

Fuel System Configuration For Start
And **NORMAL** Operation

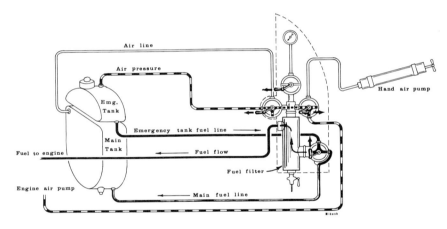

Fuel System Using **EMERGENCY** Fuel Tank
And Main Tank Refill

The right side of the cockpit shows the location of the magnetic compass which is viewed from above. The leather-covered seat slides on two rods for fore and aft adjustment. A hand air pump pressurized the fuel tanks for starting or when the engine-driven pump was inoperative.

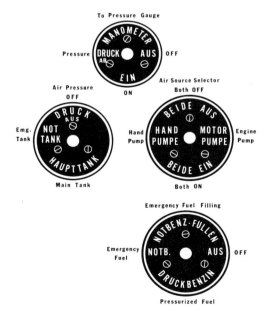

Fuel and air-selector valve position indicators located on the forward control panel in the cockpit.

against grease and that sufficient turns of screw remain to give proper lubrication. (Half turn every 10 minutes.)

(15) Hand Operated Air Pump (P)—Pump to 0.25 atmospheric pressure and lock handle.

(16) Magnetic Compass (Q)—Case level and needle swings free.

(17) Radiator Cooling Handle (R)—Full aft for maximum cooling.

(18) Compression Release Gear Handle (S)—To the right. (Vertical Position)

NOTE

This handle controls a compression relief device to ease starting the engine. In preparation for engine start, this Compression Release Gear Handle located at the face of the cam shaft is moved from left to right when viewed from the cockpit. This shifts the cam shaft so that the valve train engages another set of cams. By this action, those exhaust valves whose positions are under compression are slightly opened which provides only one-half normal compression and make the manual turning of the propeller and engine much easier. After the fuel/air mixture has been drawn into the cylinders by turning the propeller, this handle is moved back to the left and is held in that position by a detent.

(19) Flight Controls—Unlocked (T) and check freedom of movement.

(20) Throttle Handle (E)—Open slightly.

The radiator of the Albatros was in the upper wing center-section set off to the right side. It was offset to avoid restricting the pilot's forward view with the supply and return water pipes. A lever controlled by a handle regulated the air flow for cooling.

A hole was cut in the windscreen so that the engine oil that usually restricts forward vision would not hinder gunsight alignment for the pilot. The overall size of the windscreen was kept small so it would not restrict the pilot's view.

STARTING ENGINE

The engine is now ready to be started. The mechanic has just filled the primer cups of each cylinder with a mixture of oil and benzene contained in an oil can. He then pulls the Compression Release Gear Handle from the right to the left. After climbing down the ladder, he calls out "*aus*" (off). This means that the pilot should check that the ignition key handle is in place, and in the O (off) position. This is confirmed by responding to him with "*aus*." The mechanic turns the propeller 6 complete revolutions which draws the priming fuel into each of the cylinders. On the ladder once again, he moved the Compression Release Gear Handle back to the right, climbs down and moves himself and the ladder off to the side and calls out "*frei*" (free).

Pilot's response is "*frei*" and the magneto key switch is turned to the M1 (left magneto) position. Dropping the left hand to the Starting Magneto (D), its crank is turned as rapidly as possible. This starting magneto produces electricity only when the hand crank is turned. The electricity flows to the starting brush on the distributor arm which is only on magneto M1. This sends a continuous discharge of sparks across the spark plug at the cylinder

To supplement the wooden structures used as hangars, World War I aircraft were commonly housed in tent hangars as seen in the background at this German airfield. The early Albatros D.V in the foreground looks unusual without the fuselage markings and colors so common to aircraft of this period. (Peter M. Bowers)

whose piston has already passed the upper dead center. This reduces the possibility of the propeller kicking back. As the fuel in the cylinder is ignited, the engine suddenly turns and starts.

The cranking of the starting magneto need only be for a few turns, for the start (if it is going to start with this cycle) will be immediate and the other cylinders fire on their own through the engine-driven magnetos. With the engine running, the engine-driven air pump supplies air pressure to the selected fuel tank for fuel flow to the carburetor.

BEFORE TAKE OFF

Remain at the parking line to allow engine oil to warm. There is no temperature or oil pressure gauge for this system. Engine warm-up is begun at 200 to 250 rpm for about 5 to 10 minutes. After that time, the rpm can be increased to 600 by advancing the throttle. The magneto switch is then turned to the M2 (right magneto) position. If both ignition systems are operating correctly, there will be no increase or decrease in rpm. Place magneto switch to position 2, for running on both magnetos. Move Spark Control Handle to the halfway point and advance throttle to increase rpm to 800.

Signal the mechanic to move to the rear of the plane to sit against the leading edge of the stabilizer. This is a precautionary measure to hold the tail down during engine run-up while at the wheel chocks. Gradually advance Spark Control Handle to fully forward position and increase throttle to full rpm. This should be 1450 rpm. Reduce to 1300 rpm for magneto check.

Select M1 magneto position and note rpm drop, then turn to M2. The rpm should be about the same for each, and engine operation should remain smooth without missing while operating on separate magnetos. Return switch to position 2 and retard the throttle to idle at 300 to 350 rpm. (The practice of going back to "Both" between individual magneto checks did not become standard until the 1940s.) Signal the mechanic to remove the wheel chocks, for we are ready to takeoff.

This could well have been the formalized procedures for preparing the Albatros for flight. Once this phase was finished mechanics would position themselves at the wing tips. As the pilot advanced the throttle and the airplane began to move, the mechanics restrained one of the wing tips to turn the airplane to the heading that the pilot wished to go initially. There were no brakes that could be used for turning, or steerable tail skid with which the pilot could turn the airplane.

"Ground handling an airplane without brakes took a lot of practice," according to Gen. Benjamin S. Kelsey, who retired after twenty-seven years as a U.S. Air Force engineer and test pilot. He recalled flying de Havilland D.H.4s and other aircraft without brakes in many situations where wing-walkers were not available. "Taxiing crosswind was the greatest challenge," the general continued. "These little round rudders on the small planes were generally ineffective at slow speed with the tail on the ground. The taxi path was a continuing arc that kept curving into the wind. A blast of power to intentionally induce a sort of ground-loop would bring the airplane across the wind and heading at an angle off from the wind. Many wing tips would drag the ground during the course of the ground loop and could be aggravated by the airplane leaning to the outside of the turn because of "soft" chock cords.

Without brakes or steerable tail skids, the Albatros D.Va and all other aircraft of this period were difficult to control on the ground. Wing-tip handlers for guiding were a necessity in confined areas. (Puglisi)

A line of Albatros D.V fighters are parked wing tip to wing tip for a swift departure. Often after engine warm-up, takeoff would begin from the parking line to ease handling difficulties. (National Archives 165-GB-6059)

Taxiing would be continued in this series of circles until reaching the desired destination on the flying field. This was a hard way to do it," General Kelsey recalled with a slight chuckle, "but in those early designs, the problems of control to be improved were those in the air, and not for operating an airplane on the ground."

Cross-controlling by putting down the aileron that was toward the turn had greater effect than the rudder for directional control while taxiing. Often, the effectiveness of the rudder could be increased by moving the stick forward and have the downward deflected elevators take some of the restraining weight off the tail skid. To add even further assistance to this, a blast from the propeller could raise the tail off the ground and the deflected rudder would have even greater turning effect. This attempt to use increased power for rudder control frequently resulted in increasing forward speed more than it affected a turn. Many of these turns were well executed, only to have the airplane continue to roll without brakes into all sorts of obstacles such as gasoline trucks, other airplanes, and fences. With these early airplanes, there was just no substitute for wingwalkers when in close quarters or in strong winds.

TAKE OFF

Take off in the Albatros was no different from any other tail-wheel/skid-equipped aircraft. Back pressure was held firmly on the stick for keeping the tail skid on the ground for directional stability. When the rudder took effect as speed increased—which could be felt from pressure on the rudder bar and some directional control response—the tail was allowed to raise and bring the plane to a more level altitude. Take-off rolls were reported to have been short, ranging from 328 to 800 feet depending on weight, type of engine, and wind velocity.

At full throttle, take-off power was obtained at 1500 rpm. As the climb to altitude was established, the water for engine cooling heated and expanded, and the excess vented overboard from the radiator that was imbedded in the center section of the top wing. This caused vapor to stream overhead and trail behind the airplane until the excess was gone. Since this was only water, caution had to be taken in very cold climates and temperatures not to let the water freeze in the radiator. This was controlled by closing the shutters on the radiator (R); water temperature was not to exceed 70° to 75°C. Since a temperature gauge was not installed, the temperature had to be judged by the pilot which was often based upon the sound of the engine.

CRUISE

When at cruising altitude, power was reduced to 1400 rpm or less. It is difficult to describe the inflight characteristics of the Albatros in comparison with other aircraft of similar size today. When Mr. Strähle was asked this question, he too was hard pressed to give a comparison despite his experience with the Albatros and many other airplanes to date. Because of this, we can assume that the Albatros had no adverse handling qualities with the exception of the possibility of exceeding its structural limitations. A tendency to spin easily was a characteristic of the type, but there was no difficulty in recovery once the proper technique was learned and applied. The Albatros was a docile airplane to fly, yet very responsive to the controls. Judging from the lines of design, this appears to have been true. Mr. Strähle further stated that the stick movements were handled easily with only one hand although the control grips were designed for two hands, and two thumb levers were provided for firing the guns.

There were no trim controls for any axis of control on the Albatros. It is safe to assume that there was always some stick force load even for level flight. Because of this, when the pilot needed both hands to free a jammed gun, a lock on the control column could be tightened to hold the pressure and allow a few moments for free hand movement.

It was not uncommon during flight, and especially in combat, that engine oil would collect on the windscreen. For this reason the size of the windscreen was kept small so that it would not be an obstacle to forward vision. The neck scarf was always a handy item with which to wipe the oil from goggles.

LANDINGS

During landing, the Albatros apparently had no unusual traits; this was not the case with some other World War I airplanes. Typical of any biplane, the upper wing restricted visibility while in the descending turn in the landing pattern, but one learned to compensate for this. Although an anomometer was sometimes attached to the right "V" wing strut to show the airspeed, the sound and feel of the airplane gave the best indication for judging the correct landing pattern and final approach airspeeds.

The best method for landing the Albatros was full stall, three-point landings, according to Cole Palen's experience in his recently built reproduction of the Albatros. Terrain for landing was not always the smoothest, and the tightly wound bungee cords that took some of the ground roll shocks were more apt to produce bounces than the more modern shock absorbers. Ground loops were frequent with inexperienced pilots due to the narrow landing gear and inadequate directional control; flight controls became ineffective with a decrease in airspeed. The Albatros, like so many other airplanes even today, had to be "flown" every moment until it was parked and the engine came to a complete stop.

Referring to the Daimler engine operation instructions again:

> The engine is stopped after a few minutes at idle by first retarding the Spark Control Handle (B). The fuel supply (L) is then turned to the *aus* (off) position, and when the propeller stops rotating, turn ignition switch (A) to *aus*, and remove key. Bleed air pressure from the fuel tanks by turning Fuel Tank Air Pressure Selector Valve (K) to *aus*.

The flight is completed, and I hope it was interesting as well as enjoyable—even though your face is coated with engine oil!

For nearly thirty years the museum's Albatros remained in storage until January 1977. It was acquired in bad condition and was not improved as the years went by. The lower right wing rests along the fuselage side.

Restoring the Albatros

One could hardly imagine a restoration of a wood and fabric airplane that would be more challenging than rebuilding the National Air and Space Museum's Albatros D.Va. This was recognized as an essential task from the day the airplane was acquired by the museum because of the important role this fighter played in World War I. Only one other aircraft remains in the world with which to document this technology. For twenty-seven years, the museum's Albatros remained in storage until time was available for this exhaustive undertaking.

During the restoration, it was often stated that it would be easier to build an all new aircraft than to restore the original structure. The objective, however, was the preservation of the original aircraft by retaining its original construction techniques. Repairing splintered wing ribs, and splicing in portions of longerons to repair rotted sections were far more time consuming and difficult than to form new parts from fresh, clean stock. Material would be replaced only as a last resort if an original part could not be repaired.

Those who worked on the Albatros can look upon the airplane with pride, knowing that it is as close to original as possible. Its plywood fuselage skin had to be replaced and its wing and tail surfaces were covered with new fabric, which gives it a "like-new" appearance even though the basic airplane dates back to 1917.

This restoration was extremely demanding and required continual effort by the two museum craftsmen assigned to the task for twenty-six months. These museum technicians were Garry Cline and Richard Horigan, both experts in this type of fabrication, and they again proved their skills in this masterpiece of restoration. These two men alone devoted 7,401 hours to restoring the Albatros. Supporting this work was the on-call assistance of other shop technicians when their specialized skills were required. Their efforts accounted for an additional 1,228 hours, making a total of 8,629 man-hours for the entire project. This came as no surprise, for this restoration was recognized as one of the most challenging to be undertaken by the National Air and Space Museum.

To begin such an undertaking, as with all restorations, a detailed plan of action was developed. This is called the "Curatorial Package," and as Curator of Aircraft for the museum it is the responsibility of this writer to develop such restoration guidelines. This plan not only briefly describes the history of the airplane so that the technicians can have a better understanding of the airplane, but it describes in great detail what the final configuration and appearance of the airplane is to be. In the case of this Albatros, it was to be restored as closely as possible to its combat configuration complete with its offensive armament and any special equipment that might have been installed. The curatorial package also points out what technical details to watch for and record while dismantling the airplane. Unusual markings found on the structure may tell something of its history and add further information on

An essential preliminary to restoration is to provide easy access to all sections of the object. The fuselage is mounted on an engine stand so that it can be rotated into any position.

For nearly the entire life of this Albatros D.Va while it was in the United States, its serial was not known since it was over-painted with yellow and green tail stripes. In time, the paint eroded, revealing its identity as D.7161/17. Note rudder leading-edge bar is in place although the remainder of the rudder is broken off.

techniques used in its manufacture. This is a form of intelligence gathering, not unlike that used in a wartime situation while analyzing a foreign aircraft.

Anticipated problem areas are also covered in the plan. In this case, the pros and cons of retaining in part or replacing the fuselage skin entirely was recorded in the plan for future reference. The decision was made to replace the skin entirely, and the method for accomplishing this was given in detail. Other factors, ranging from the degree of engine restoration that would be required, to possible sources for metric-size bracing wires, were included in this plan. Finally, an accurate description of the markings and colors, along with diagrams for application, were included along with any other source material that would aid the technicians.

No individual curator, or one museum for that matter, should presume to have all the answers for a restoration of the magnitude of this Albatros. For this reason, copies of the curatorial package were sent to five persons considered to be the most knowledgeable on Albatros details, or on the restoration of aircraft having this type of construction. The responses were rewarding and the various viewpoints often led to changes that improved the final restoration.

In most cases of aircraft restoration, a shop outline, often called "How to Do the Job" is prepared before actual restoration work is begun. This document records missing parts, describes the existing condition of various components, and explains the steps needed to be taken in the restoration. Also included are special precautions that would lead to preserving original materials and construction techniques and includes a breakdown on the estimated man-hours for major task areas. Using this work program as a guide, those restoring the airplane can plan and coordinate their efforts so that all major components, materials, and the like, can be programmed into an orderly work schedule. This time-consuming inspection and outline of work was accomplished by Joe Fichera, who has been in the restoration business for many years. The time spent on this phase of planning is well justified for the overall effort.

The areas of work to be accomplished for each aircraft is broken down by the museum into six categories for record-keeping purposes and is often used in assigning work responsibilities to technicians. In general, these subject areas are: fuselage, cockpit, engine, wings, empennage, and finish and assembly. For the purpose of describing this restoration, these subject areas will be covered in this order.

Fuselage

At the onset, this fuselage was a literal "basket case." It appeared there was little that could be done except to use its parts as patterns, retaining and using some of the best components, and start anew; however, this would defeat the purpose of preserving the original structure. Museum technician Richard Horigan, well skilled in aviation woodworking techniques, took on the fuselage project which became a challenge to his ability to accomplish the virtually impossible.

For several months, the work continued with little visible progress. Rich's time was absorbed in patternmaking and in the building of forms and molds to match the original contours for the replacement skin. Without visible progress on the structure, a project of this nature can become discouraging to the builder; if this was the case, Rich did not let it show.

The area of greatest deterioration on the Albatros was the 2-mm-thick plywood skin on the semimonocoque fuselage. Over the years preceding this

One of the first steps was cleaning the fuselage interior of the years of dirt accumulation. After cleaning, this view from the engine mounts rearward shows the makeshift formers at mid-section along the bottom of the fuselage.

Restoration of the fuselage began from the aft section. Each piece of skin was carefully removed to serve as a pattern and reference for other details. The upper and lower fins were integral parts of the fuselage.

restoration we had considered the possibility of removing the many plywood panels separately and impregnating them with Wood Rot Cure, an epoxy penetrant, to strengthen and preserve this original, yet deteriorated, wood. Areas of the skin panels that had literally rotted away could be built up with this epoxy material. Although this was possible, it was recognized that the finished fuselage would not look as it did originally, but instead would be a patchwork of old material in contrast with new and filled-in skin areas. This left no choice but to re-skin the entire fuselage.

Here was an airplane built sixty years before this restoration began and in another part of the world. Where would plywood of this grade and metric size be found today? After a search of aviation products that covered many parts of the world, thin plywood in metric measurement and similar grades of birch was found to be produced in Finland. An order was placed for this material and when received, it was nearly a perfect match to the plywood found on the fuselage.

The original 3-ply birch plywood varied from 2 mm to approximately 2.5 mm over most of the fuselage, and two pieces on each side of the engine bay measured 3 mm. The lower tail skid fin was a double thickness of 2 mm material. Except for the 3 mm plywood skin on the sides of the nose, 2 mm material was used throughout the fuselage.

In reworking the fuselage, there was no way that all the skin could be removed and replaced at one time. The alignment and rigidity of the fuselage were dependent on the strength given to it by the skin. Therefore, only a few sections at a time could be removed and replaced with new panels before moving on to the next area.

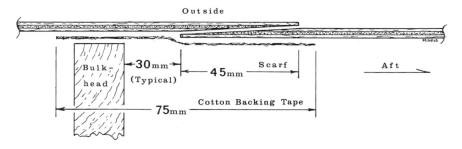

Typical fuselage-skin scarf joint. Not to scale.

During this process, a feature of this fuselage construction was discovered that is not apparent when looking at photographs or even fuselage drawings which are usually incorrect. The skin mating lines do not fall at the location of the fuselage formers as the drawings imply and as would naturally be expected. The reason was first revealed while viewing a motion-picture film that was made at the Albatros factory during World War I. In a brief glimpse there appeared to be entire fuselage sides being carried to production areas. A study of the original Albatros skin showed that the top, bottom, and two sides were pre-shaped and glued as four major units and then attached as large panels to the fuselage frame. This forming of the skin may well have been accomplished through the use of large molds possibly cast from cement as Lockheed did with the Vega. In the process, steam-softened rectangular plywood skin panels were pressed in the mold and glued together with 50 mm scarf joints with the splice reinforced by a strip of heavy-weave linen cloth glued to the inside. While Roland and Pfalz employed male molds for this process, details on the inside skin face of the Albatros fuselage imply that

The first piece of the structure to go back on the airplane was installed in late March 1977. This end piece of the fuselage supports the stabilizer.

It was a memorable day when the initial piece of new skin was attached to the fuselage located at the base of the fin. This was April 6, 1977. Richard Horigan who did the fuselage restoration applies the final touch of sanding before moving along to the next piece.

The skin at the rear of the fuselage had complicated compound curves for smooth contours with the top and bottom fins and stabilizer. Molds for these pieces were fabricated as shown here using the fuselage former contours and dimensions of the original skin pieces as guides. The top portion required seven pieces, and the lower side required eight molded plywood pieces.

female molds were used. On the museum's Albatros, many edges of this cloth were found sandwiched between the bulkheads and the skin, further supporting the theory that the cloth was attached over the splice while held in the mold which was female and before the skin was secured to the fuselage structure.

This technique complicated the restoration of the Albatros. Since the molds could not be re-created with the assurance they would produce the original contours accurately, the skin pieces had to be fitted separately to the fuselage structure. Since the skin splices were located in areas away from the support of formers, this often required the temporary insertion of a false former to provide stability and the correct shape when joining skin panels.

This re-skinning process had to be started at the rear of the fuselage due to the direction of the scarf laps. Unfortunately, this area was the most difficult, as fifteen differently shaped pieces in this tail section had to be molded individually to their unique contours. The question was asked whether plywood could be formed into compound curves. "If the Germans could do it, I can do it," Rich commented—and he did.

Before removing the old skin in this area for molding new pieces, templates were made of the curves. These were transformed into wood diaphragms and attached in a box-frame arrangement, for both a male and female form. The area between these diaphragms were then filled with plaster of Paris to make a continuous contoured form. The plywood to be formed was then placed in a steam box for from five to ten minutes to be softened. It was then clamped between the two halves of the mold for four days, then clamped on the fuselage frame for one day of final drying.

After a few necessary alterations were made to the molds to compensate for hidden stresses, the desired compound shapes were obtained. This was a slow, arduous operation, but this insistence on perfection got the repair of the fuselage off to an excellent start. The other panels, cut to exact dimensions of the originals, could then be formed directly on the fuselage.

Plaster of Paris and body putty make up the surface between the contour baffles of the male and female mold. Richard Horigan removed the newly formed skin from the mold after it was allowed to dry for several days.

The freshly formed skin panel, seen being removed from the mold in the picture (above), was attached at the left base of the fin. Cloth strip backing at the top edge helped strengthen the seam. This was a feature of the Albatros semi-monocoque fuselage design.

This mold was for the lower fuselage skin which is just forward of the vertical fin. After a thorough steaming for five to ten minutes in a closed box, the 2-mm 3-ply birch plywood was sandwiched between the two molds and allowed to dry for four to five days.

As in the original manner, most sections were attached with screws at their corners. Rows of nails and glue were used to further hold the skin to the formers and longerons. For this restoration, the skin was first held in place by the screws positioned into the original screw holes with the aide of a blind rivet-hole locator. The structure outline was then traced on the inside face of the skin and then the panel was removed. A centerline for the nails was drawn within the penciled lines of the structure and evenly marked for the nails at ¾-inch intervals. A #60 drill-size hole was made at each mark. Glue was applied to the fuselage formers, the skin again screwed back to its earlier location and ½-inch #18 steel cement-coated aircraft nails were driven through each hole which resulted in a perfect alignment of the nails. New nails had to be used for attaching the skin, for to have restored the old nails in these small quantities for this long de-rusting and preservation process would have been impractical.

These before and after pictures of the rear of the fuselage, provide a graphic example of the extremely deteriorated condition from which a "like-new" Albatros emerged. Except for new skin, the basic structure components were cleaned, repaired, and retained in place.

The internal details of the aft fuselage include the metal attachment fittings for wires and turnbuckles that add support to the tail-skid attachment points in the ventral fin. Four bolts went to a plate on the outside of the skin for added strength. Side longerons stop midpoint between the two formers and have a side spacer block which attaches to the stabilizer root rib when in place.

This is the interior view of the fin base area joining the fuselage after new skin was attached. Note factory inspection stamp in center of former.

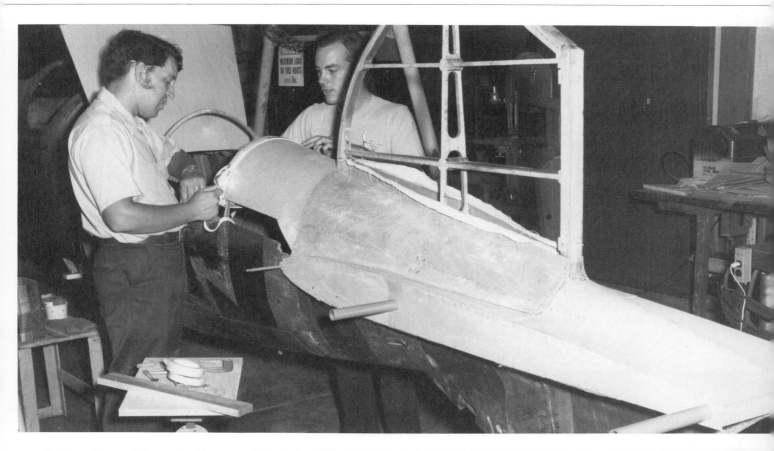

Glue is the primary skin application method, supported by light screws and nails. Richard Horigan aided by Garry Cline apply a compression strap to hold one section of skin while the glue dries.

For added protection to the new skin, two coats of polyurethane varnish were added to the inside surface before it was attached to the structure. Spar varnish was the original material used by the Albatros factory. The surface area to be glued was not varnished as this would have inhibited the holding quality of the glue.

The stabilizer root ribs were made up of three pieces; the inner core of 3-mm poplar with lightening holes, and capped on both sides with 2-mm birch plywood. A 6-mm-square strip frame on the inside face of the rib added more gluing surface for the skin.

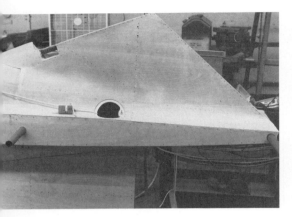

The ventral fin, shown here inverted for easier accessibility, was the only area with a double covering of 2-mm plywood for strength in supporting the tail skid. Due to this double skin, this access opening has a recessed lip for a flush-fitting cover.

Since the top and bottom skin were applied first before the sides in the original manufacture, the edge of the old side panels had to be cut away from the longerons to facilitate this reassembly. As few of the skin panels as possible were removed at one time in order to retain fuselage alignment.

Before a new skin panel is glued in place, the internal structure is marked on the inside and lead nail holes are drilled for a straight alignment on the outside. Note the beveled skin edges for a scarf joint, yet the skin does not mate over a former.

Nylon ropes served as temporary control cables while the skinning process took place which simplified routing the cables through the fuselage when it was fully covered. Note the temporary former held by C-clamps to support the skin and to give a true contour when attaching the next piece of skin.

This is the area of the cockpit in an inverted position. The tear-shaped areas for three holes on the inside fuselage formers hold the pilot's seat rails.

Every size, shape, and description of clamps were utilized for making a tightly glued joint along the skin edge. This is the area aft of the cockpit.

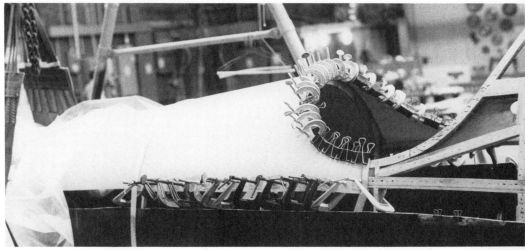

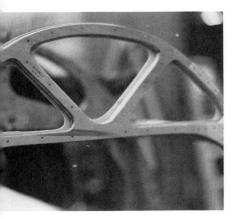

This reinforced former at the bottom of the cockpit has imprinted on it "Repaired 2/8/78." All new material is marked so that in time a differentiation can be made between new and original material. Repair to the former was made without removing it, and further trimming has to be done.

Trying to duplicate the original adhesives would not have had technical value. Instead, modern adhesives, such as Weldwood plastic resin glue, were used in this restoration for greater strength and durability. Gluing had obviously been the primary method for joining materials, while screws and nails were secondary.

Restoring the interior structure of the fuselage was nearly as demanding as the re-skinning. Ideally, this work should have been done with the fuselage completely unskinned. Instead, only small sections at a time could be cleaned and repaired where longerons and formers were exposed by the removal of single panels of skin. Some of the formers at the belly of the fuselage were completely rotted away, while others had been poorly patched for exhibit purposes many years ago and all the rotted wood had to be replaced.

The restored interior of the skin and structure was covered with two coats of spar varnish. As each section was completed, it was brush-painted from the outside through the next newly opened section.

New gussets replace the broken away members of the fuselage cross brace. Clear Lexan pads are used for see-through assurance of proper positioning of parts since glue does not adhere to this type of material.

This close-up view shows a typical 50-mm scarf joint used for the fuselage skin. The heavy-weave cotton fabric torn in strips about 75 mm wide for lap strength was often sandwiched between the former and the skin. This was the result of these skin shells being preformed and glued together before being attached to the fuselage frame.

Cross-member spars for the lower wing mount were built as part of the fuselage-former structure. Steel straps tied the two opposite wing-spar fittings together. Note the imbedded ground wire, off center along the longeron.

This picture shows details of how the half-completed lower wing attachment stub was built. The next step was to attach the butt rib. Both the upper and lower surfaces of this wing root were plywood covered.

End view of wing root at fuselage. The two lugs are for flying wires and the two holes with bushings guide the aileron control cables into the lower wing.

The bottom fuselage skin forms a clean line, broken only by inspection openings and drain-hole grommets. Leading edge of closest skin has already been beveled back 50 mm for the next scarf joint.

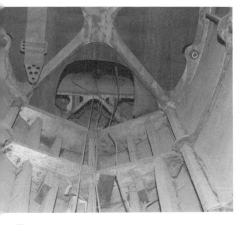

Two comparison photos show the same area of the fuselage before and after restoration. The photo above faces forward to the rear of the cockpit that is closed with a canvas bulkhead. Photo at right is looking aft before bulkhead is installed. Cross rods in foreground support the pilot's seat.

Before and after comparison views show the same right-side area of the nose. Makeshift spacers between first and second formers were eliminated during the restoration. All screw slots are aligned horizontally throughout the fuselage as they were originally.

This close-up shows many structural details such as the landing-gear fittings to the fuselage and the recessed area of the wing root through which the landing gear passes. The wing root is plywood covered, both top and bottom.

An outline of the fuselage structure was drawn on the inside of each piece of skin while being held in place with a few alignment screws. Centerlines were then drawn and #60-size holes were drilled through which nails will be driven.

The nearly finished fuselage was rolled over for adding final details. Forward and rear gun mounts are visible in this view.

It was interesting to discover ground wires literally imbedded into the fuselage structure. They were placed in grooves along the outside of the upper and lower longerons so that when the skin was applied, they were concealed in the structure. The ground wire routing was from the engine mount, along the longeron to the lower wing-spar reinforcements and on to the tail-post tube and horizontal stabilizer. The wire along the upper longeron connects to the top wing-strut fittings and the ground is carried by the metal struts to the top wing which also has a ground wire.

Weeks turned into months and piece by piece of precisely sized plywood replaced the old, moving from the tail to the nose. Before dirt or discoloration could take place, several coats of spar varnish were applied to the completed plywood surface as was the practice in German production. Early forms of varnish had a yellow cast which resulted in a warm transparent straw color for the fuselage, while modern varnish with less discoloration had left this fuselage a little lighter perhaps than when originally manufactured. Experience gained in finishing this fuselage indicates that we should have added a tint to the varnish with raw sienna or burnt umber to darken the plywood slightly.

With the engine installed and the fuselage resting on its landing gear, this phase of the restoration, after twenty months of work, was completed. This included detailing of the cockpit and engine restoration.

These two views of the Albatros cockpit show the degree to which this restoration was carried. Many parts in this area were missing and either had to be acquired or fabricated. It is difficult to believe this is the same aircraft.

Cockpit

Restoring a cockpit is usually an unpleasant task due to the cramped working space and the many wires, tubes, and accessories that make cleaning so very difficult. In the case of the Albatros, however, this section was quite different. To begin with, there were very few components compared with later cockpit interiors, and all were able to be temporarily removed for restoration. Also, with the fuselage skin removed, the internal details of the fuselage structure were easily accessible for cleaning and necessary repair. When new skin was attached to the fuselage structure, this naturally gave a clean, like-new interior.

The cockpit and its equipment are of vital concern to the National Air and Space Museum in the restoring of any aircraft. It is here that the technology available to the pilot for the operation of the aircraft can be observed and studied. In the case of this Albatros, researches can now find every detail in its place, just as it was when the airplane was combat-ready in World War I.

A study had to be made of how the various systems components operated so they could be properly connected and restored on a like-new and workable condition. These components and their functions are far different from those in use today and have been described in the earlier segment about this Albatros.

A number of cockpit items were missing and had to be replaced—no simple task for an airplane out of production for such a long period. Fortunately, the replacement booster starter magneto was obtained from Joseph M. DeFiore, an expert restorer of early aircraft in his own right, and owner of Aerotique, Inc., in Enid, Oklahoma. DeFiore's particular interest and experience is with World War I aircraft, and he was helpful more than once during the restoration of this Albatros.

From the museum's collection of vintage instruments, a fuel gauge was located to replace one of the missing items. Although the size and mechanism

The two ammunition cans are different in design. Shown here in place in the forward end of the cockpit before restoration, they were removed for repair and corrosion control.

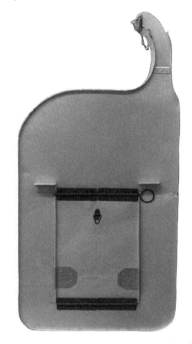

The left ammunition can repaired and ready to be installed.

of this instrument matched the original type, the dial was graduated differently. John Siske of the museum's Exhibit Department undertook the task of recreating a new face. He photographed the old dial which contained many items such as the manufacturer's stylized name and other markings common to the required face. He used these details to develop a new dial face to match pictures showing the correct design. The museum's Exhibit Department is often called upon to apply its myriad capabilities to small details of this type.

Ammunition cans and their feed chutes located in front of the pilot's knees were cleaned of corrosion and repaired; however, a new expended cartridge belt container had to be fabricated. Details like this container and other missing parts were often provided by Bob Waugh of South Australia, who made frequent reference to the D.Va in Australia for sketching these details. Over the years preceding this restoration, Francis P. Garove of Baltimore, Maryland, had taken a deep interest in the museum's Albatros and had gathered this type of material from such friends of the museum as Bob Waugh, Peter M. Grose, Peter M. Bowers, Ed Ferko, the late William Puglisi, the Australian War Memorial Museum, and others. This combined effort provided many of the needed details for ready reference in the fabrication of parts and saved considerable research time for the museum staff.

One of the embossed identifying valve placards located in the cockpit was also missing from the museum's Albatros. To replace this, David R. McMullen, who was in the process of building his own reproduction Albatros in

The right ammunition can. Note upper hinged door with latch for access in feeding belts.

The spent cartridge chutes were complicated assemblies. These original items were repaired and used again.

With ammunition boxes in place in the restored Albatros cockpit, a missing cartridge-belt container was fabricated and installed to the left of center. Although many details are visible in this picture, this cockpit is relatively simple compared to later machines.

Details of the right-hand machine-gun mount can be clearly seen in this view of the partially completed cockpit.

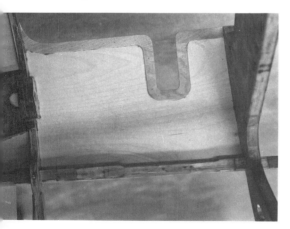

Edges of the cockpit area skin have a double thickness for strength. This is the detailing around the slot for the left-hand spent cartridge chute.

Photos were taken of every assembly before restoration was begun to serve as a record during the reassembly. This right-side view of the control column shows many of its details. The control-column locking arm in the center is bent and broken.

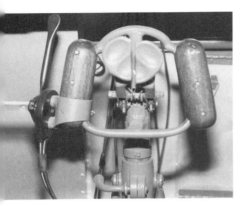

Close-up view of the control-column hand grips. Two gun-firing thumb buttons are in the center and the throttle is on the left grip.

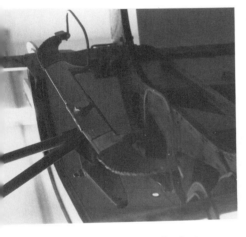

Rudder bar details show the foot straps on either side and the control horn below.

This detail photo looking forward over the engine shows the position of the two MG 08/15 machine guns. The handle in the center of the picture is the compression-release gear handle and in the foreground center are the interrupter-gear flexible drive shafts from the engine for synchronizing the machine guns for firing through the propeller arc.

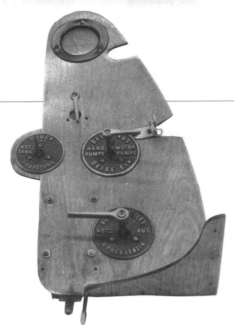

Front side of the fuel/air control panel which is located on the right side of the forward cockpit area. A newly fabricated label plate for the top control is not in place in this view.

Rear side of the fuel/air control panel shows the multi-purpose control valve. The main barrel is the fuel filter.

California, offered a spare example that he had cast for his project. Going one step further at the museum, Rich Horigan used this casting as a mold and made an aluminum impression that more closely matched the originals in the cockpit and thus was able to return the casting to McMullen. A look inside the cockpit reveals little evidence that one of these placards is not an original. Museum records on this Albatros restoration, however, list this item as a replacement and not an original piece.

The restored Mercedes D.IIIa 180-hp engine in the museum's Albatros is a shining example of this outstanding and reliable World War I aircraft engine. This 6-cylinder engine is water cooled.

Engine

It was with some regret that this Mercedes engine was placed back into the Albatros, for it is an interesting engine to examine, especially after being so beautifully restored. Many of its unique details are difficult to detect when shrouded by the fuselage, cowling, and a mass of plumbing.

For this restoration, the engine was completely disassembled to be inspected for damage, thoroughly cleaned, and properly preserved both inside as well as outside. As the cylinders were removed, it was discovered that each was stamped with a letter to show their location on the engine block, starting at the front with A through F. Intake valves and cylinder hold-down dogs were also lettered to correspond with respective cylinders. This was particularly noteworthy, since numbers were also stamped on the cylinder block at the base of each cylinder, but these referred to the firing order. Details of this nature are recorded during pre-restoration inspection whenever possible, but in this case grease and caked dirt had hidden these details until the engine was disassembled and cleaned.

Every part of the Mercedes was disassembled, cleaned, and preserved. Richard Horigan begins the task of rebuilding the engine by preparing the lower engine block to receive the crank shaft.

These before- and after-restoration comparison photos were taken in the same general area above the engine. The temporarily inserted rod shows the path of the bullet that first penetrated the machine-gun mount, grazed the emergency fuel tank, and struck the magneto. Except for replacing this magneto, battle damage was not altered.

The two-barrel carburetor on the left side of the engine, shows that each will feed three cylinders. The steel induction pipes are wound with asbestos cord and bound with tape. Dummy spark plugs patterned after an authentic plug for this engine are used until the original type can be located.

The engine was missing a number of parts that no longer are available. Museum machinist Harvey Napier re-created new parts by using a duplicate as a pattern. It takes a skilled eye to determine which is the new part.

As an example of the attention in cleaning and preserving that is given to an engine such as this Mercedes, the following is a paragraph from "How to Do the Job" that pertains to engine parts restoration:

4. Clean all aluminum parts in aluminum cleaner rather than sandblasting to maintain a natural aluminum appearance. Sandblast all cylinders and rusty steel parts. Remove valves and valve springs and "blue" valve springs with gun bluing chemical. Remove all carbon on valve faces and parts by sandblasting with glass beads. Preserve all steel parts with CRC 3-36 [this commercial product has the appearance of oil when applied but becomes semidry as a lasting protective coating]. Soak crankshaft, connecting rods and pistons in carbon remover.

This single paragraph describes several of the processes that are used to ensure the thoroughness of this or any other restoration project.

The list of missing parts on this engine was long. Some could be fabricated by modifying existing materials such as ignition harnesses and stock hoses. Metal parts including the rocker cover on the No. 5 cylinder, compression release valve on cylinders 2, 5, and 6, along with many knobs, hold-down clamps and other intricate items had to be machined by the shop machinist, Harvey Napier. Each piece that Napier turned out was a work of machining art—an exact reproduction of the original.

Only one of the original spark plugs was with the engine, and no replacements for the other eleven could be found. While the search continued, Harvey machined dummies out of two pieces of steel for each plug, and the porcelain areas were painted white.

Once again, David McMullen provided an important item by replacing the missing Bosch ZH6 Model 21 magneto on the right side that had been hit by a bullet on the airplane's last flight and later was removed by the victor or the victim.

Just looking at the completed engine gave everyone a strong desire to see and hear this Mercedes run and to bring it back to life once again. This would

Two views of the restored Mercedes 180-hp engine for the Albatros before being installed. From the outside, the engine appears ready for run-up on the test stand; however, a preservative coating of CRC 3-36 and Soft Seal lines all the internal walls for lasting protection. This material can be removed and replaced with engine oil and the proper grease should the need ever arise to run the engine.

The left rear area of the engine contains the left magneto, known then as M1. This magneto has a special wiper arm used exclusively for engine starting. This supplies spark to the cylinder having a piston that has just passed the top of the compression stroke.

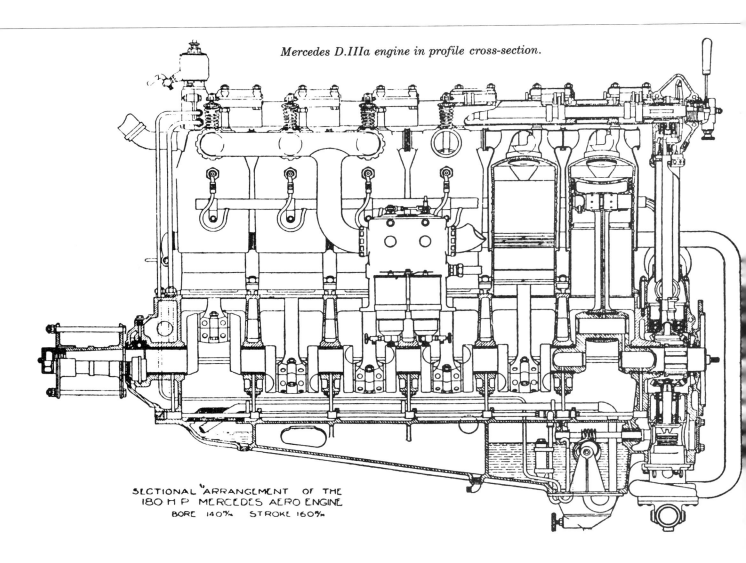

Mercedes D.IIIa engine in profile cross-section.

This view of the 160-hp Mercedes engine (right) is included for comparison with the 180-hp engine (above) since the two are often falsely identified. The most noticeable difference is that on the 180-hp engine, the water pump is directly behind the oil pump and is attached to the lower part of the crankcase. For the 160-hp Mercedes, the water pump is higher on the tower shaft which connects the cam shaft with the crankcase. This engine has a more pronounced lower crankcase and does not taper as much toward the nose as the 180-hp Mercedes. (Joseph M. DeFiore)

The Garuda propeller logo was carefully constructed from early Garuda advertisements and photographs. Decal color separations are reproduced in Part IV of this book.

The airfoil-shaped radiator was completely disassembled and each tube was cleaned inside and out and coated with a preservative. The outer finish is silver. The small cone facing forward into the air stream provided pressure for the radiator.

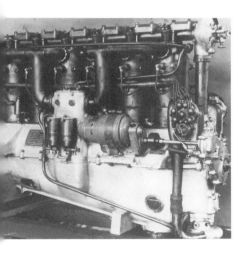

This view of another 180-hp Mercedes has a generator and gear drive mounted on the left side of the engine block. This was not true of all 180-hp Mercedes engines, for this accessory was possibly required on bombers where lighting and radio equipment were carried. The discovery of mounting lugs for the generator, or finding the generator installed, often resulted in falsely identifying with this feature as being 200-hp Mercedes engines. (Joseph M. DeFiore)

The fuel tanks were mounted directly behind the engine. The filler cap in the right foreground is for the main tank which is mounted directly below the emergency tank seen here. Its filler neck protrudes through a passage in the upper emergency fuel tank.

not be practical since all internal surfaces are coated with a mixture of CRC 3-36 and Soft Seal for preservation. This material sprayed inside gives a rust- and corrosion-resistant coating on all surfaces, yet remains soft enough that if the propeller is turned for alignment, the material will not be fully scraped off the cylinder walls and other areas of wear. Nothing is ever done to permanently inhibit the engine from being run again, should the need arise, but in the meantime, every preservation precaution has been taken.

The Garuda propeller was found to be in a very poor condition. The laminations had come loose at nearly every joining surface and both blades were nicked and one tip was missing. It was far more practical to have this propeller restoration handled by a contractor specializing in this type work. Consequently, Kern Weinhold of the Sensenich Brothers propeller factory and repair facility at Lancaster, Pennyslvania, accomplished this phase of the restoration.

Unfortunately, during final assembly of the Albatros, it was discovered that the propeller spinner would not fit on this propeller. After further inspection, it was found that this propeller was for a 160-hp Mercedes engine and not for this 180-hp engine and spinner. At some point over the years an exchange of propellers had taken place. Until the correct pitched propeller can be obtained or constructed, the 160-hp propeller is installed with a fiberglass spinner so that the original spinner did not have to be altered to make it fit. Inside the original spinner was found marked with pencil "7222/17" and "2888 Propulsor," (trade name) along with "4711" stamped on the outside edge.

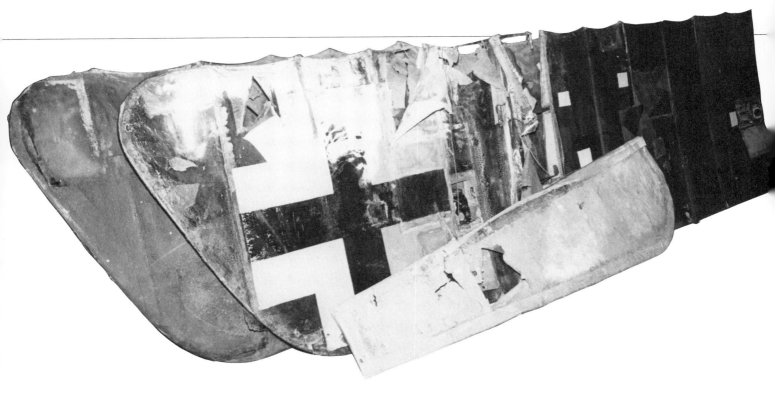

The lower wings of the Albatros in storage show the original straight-sided German cross used after March 20, 1918. This design was not duplicated on the restoration as the earlier marking style found on the fuselage was followed. These wings are probably not original to the fuselage. The lozenge fabric is also apparent here.

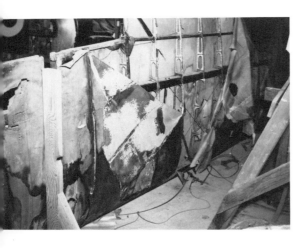

This shows the condition of the top wing when the restoration began. Since much of the fabric remained on the three wings over the years, the many parts that broke or came unglued were not lost.

Wings

While the foregoing was taking place, Garry Cline undertook the restoration of the wings. As the rotted fabric was carefully removed and set aside for future reference and pattern needs, the structure took on the appearance of a mass of disjointed sticks. At this point, the wings appeared to be an impossible task much as the fuselage had been at the start. They appeared suitable only for patterns. With the confident smile that never seems to fade from Cline, he began the fourteen-month task of restoring these three wings; upper, lower left, and lower right.

Starting with the left lower wing, the plan was to complete it before the right wing was altered in any way. Thus, one could always serve as a pattern for the other. As glue seemed to have deteriorated at all joints, the entire wing structure had to be fully disassembled, each rib repaired, and the wing reassembled. The one advantage of this time-consuming task was that it allowed for the thorough cleaning and repair of each part, particularly the box spars whose 3 mm birch plywood webbing had delaminated in many places. In fact, the top wing spars were broken at approximately midpoint of the wing. In this disassembly, the original nails were removed; most were able to be restored and were used again during the rebuilding process. The restoration of the nails consisted of soaking them first in a hot alkaline rust stripper and then a hot phosphate solution, followed by a dipping in linseed oil as a preservative.

All wood used in the restoration of the wings was in metric sizes. Ash, basswood (linden) and long-leaf pine were used in the original wing, and the same type of woods were used for replacement parts. According to Joe Fichera, one of the senior restorers at the museum's facility, the current FAA Manual 43.13-1 contains good repair procedures to follow, for few changes have been made in wood repair methods since World War I. All splices that were needed for inserting new and replacement structural members were 15 to 1 for hard woods and 10 to 1 for soft woods.

Each wing had to be totally disassembled for restoration. These are the top wing spars webbed with 2-mm 3-ply birch plywood, some of which had to be removed to make internal repairs. Garry Cline restored all three of the Albatros wings, a job that required 2,226 hours.

A before-and-after view of the top wing shows the amount of restoration required. Original pieces were retained as much as possible and spliced with new material where needed. Replacement parts were clearly stamped with the date and that the repair was made by NASM.

In the area of the aileron-horn cutouts, the wing spar and wing rib caps had deteriorated badly. Many of the rib cap strips had to be replaced with new ash wood, all finished to metric sizes. Original and replacement gussets are 3-mm 3-ply plywood. New parts are stamped as replacement or repaired parts and then dated.

This view of the upper wing at the inboard corner of the aileron cutout shows the attachment of rib number 7R to the auxiliary spar. String lacings hold a woven cotton reinforcing tape to which the fabric is then fastened. Note the .050-inch-diameter ground wire threaded through the ribs. This is a 1 × 7 twisted-wire cable.

Almost every wing rib requires some type of repair, from merely regluing loose portions, to ribs with so much of their structure broken or missing that a nearly new rib had to be built. No completely new rib was used, for each one had some original piece included. Garry Cline fabricated jigs for this work to ensure accurate and constant contours. This worked well for the lower wings, but to everyone's surprise, a number of ribs on the upper wing had variations in camber especially in the area of the radiator. It seemed apparent that this could have been done to compensate for the radiator which may not have matched the intended airfoil. Since this was an unrecorded structural and technical find, Cline made tracings of the various rib forms which have been reproduced for future reference in this publication.

Two views, before and after restoration, of the upper wing, left aileron cutout area. Pictures of the unrestored aircraft show progress, but primarily serve as references to the original construction techniques that must be duplicated.

Unlike the top wing, few lightening holes were cut in the lower wing ribs. All ribs are linden wood (bass), and not plywood. Garry Cline is shown here reassembling the ribs around the lower wing spar using templates for retaining rigid and accurate contours.

The bow at the upper mid-span cutout location was rotted beyond repair; however, this piece remained useful as a pattern for the construction of a new piece.

Having prepared a form around which to fabricate a new bow, three strips of ash cut to match the original pieces were glued together and held by clamps until dry. Some inside areas of the strips have already been cut out to ease final routing of the finished assembly.

After the glue has cured and the bow is set, a groove was carved on the face toward the inside of the wing before the outside surface was carved to a rounded shape.

Reassembling the top wing after repairs have been made to the many parts was a tedious alignment task. Weldwood glue was the basic attaching device and, as in the original German-made assembly, wooden shims were required at spar cap-strip joints.

This early stage in the reassembly of the top wing-tip area shows the wing-tip inner contour strip that joins the front spar with the rear spar. Pieces of each rib to be added later in the assembly were temporarily taped to the inner structure of the respective ribs.

Bottom view of lower right wing-tip structure at the leading edge. Original reinforcement tapes to which the fabric covering was sewn were either 4 mm or 7 mm wide.

Reassembling the wing became an arduous task in that care had to be taken not to induce a warp into the structure as the wings were rebuilt. Instead of completing each rib with its numerous small pieces, complications arose on the top wing which required assembling each rib around the two spars. This became necessary to eliminate the need for removing the permanently attached fittings and glued reinforcement blocks that would otherwise hinder slipping into place each completed rib over the end of the spar. Some ingenious jigs, templates, and methods evolved from this unorthodox reassembly.

The Germans were very methodical with their own markings of these wing ribs. From the center rib on the upper wing, and the butt ribs of the lower wings, each was numbered consecutively outward to the wing tips. Ribs left of the centerline were marked on the left side, and conversely for the right.

Wing-tip bows had become badly damaged over the years, but their outlines could be traced for use in making templates and fixtures to reconstruct them to their original shape. At first it was thought that these tip bows were made of three laminations of wood. Instead, two parallel cuts were made lengthwise in this wing-tip member, forming what appeared to be three separate strips. This made the bend much easier, and the strips were then glued together. This was only done in the area of the wing-tip bow where the bend was to take place. They were then routed on the inside of this curved area to reduce weight.

As with many aircraft designs of that period, the wing trailing edge consisted of a piano wire approximately 1 mm in diameter, attached to the back tip of each rib by a simple aluminum boxlike clip. Normally, this wire was stretched to about 100 pounds tension according to Joe Fichera, who found this reference in a manual for repairs on Jennys. Since this Albatros was not to fly and was to last indefinitely, this tension was lowered to 30 to 50 pounds to reduce structural stresses. This wire had to be taut enough that when the fabric was applied and tightened, the scallops would be even with no tendency to bend upward or downward.

This right rear view of the lower right wing tip shows the restored structure ready for fabric covering. A slot in the wing rib where it butts against the wing spar fits over the small wood block for the correct vertical alignment. Fabric strip from the rib cap forward was 22-mm cotton tape, and a 150-mm-wide strip was doped to the wing leading edge as chafe strips.

A double-contour forming jig for the leading-edge cap strip formed the 2-mm plywood before it was attached to the wing. The original material measured closer to 1.5 mm. Note how the two leading edges lock one another in place. Overnight drying set the curves.

These four photographs show factory ink stamp markings and inspector's names with stamps found on the lower wing ribs and inside the wing spar. Ribs are numbered consecutively from the butt rib outward with numbers on the left face for the left wing. Markings of this type were found throughout the entire structure of the aircraft.

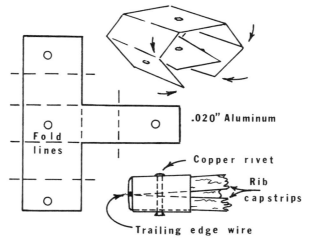

Wing-rib trailing-edge wire clip. Pattern is full size.

The front and rear top wing spars were held by seven black-painted steel compression bars with turnbuckle-adjusted cross wires in between. These made rib installation difficult, but maintained true alignment. Shown here are ribs one through seven, left.

Close-up detail of compression-bar attachment bracket to wing spar and alignment wire with brass turnbuckle. Original black material was more like a coating of dark preservative, but black enamel was a suitable preservative and was substituted for this restoration.

Corrosion control is as important in restoring wood and fabric aircraft as it is in all-metal aircraft. Every steel and aluminum part of the Albatros was processed through Will Powell's chemical treatment facility in the same building where these restorations take place. The type of metal, its thickness, and type of damage must be taken into consideration with each part to determine the correct process for preservation.

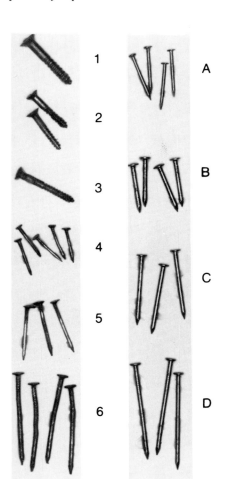

This photograph shows the actual size of nails and screws used throughout the structure of the Albatros. The primary structure bond in most cases was glue, therefore, nails and screws were used basically to hold the parts while the glue cured and provided additional strength. Since each wing was fully disassembled and rebuilt, it was possible to reuse many of the original nails by having them soaked in hot alkaline rust stripper, and then a hot phosphate solution, followed by dipping in linseed oil as a preservative. Listed below, the numbered hardware is original German material and the lettered nails are American made, which were used as supplements and replacements where needed.

1. *Flush-head steel screws used to attach steel fittings onto wing spars.*
2. *Flush-head steel screws used for attaching wing leading edge to nose ribs and other locations within the wing, such as, cap strips to spar locations, wing-tip bow attachment, and center bow on top wing. Aluminum screws of this size were predominant throughout the wing structure. (No brass nails or screws were found on the aircraft.)*
3. *Steel screws used in small number at random within the wing.*
4. *Steel nails used on wing leading-edge skin for attachment to spar. Also used along rib cage into plywood webbing and to hold cloth rib-stitch tapes to ribs where it is looped and tied with cord.*
5. *Steel nails used where suited for structure, primarily at wing-tip web gussets.*
6. *Steel nails used primarily for attaching filler blocks onto wing-tip spar and rib-angle junctions.*

A. *American ½-inch, No. 20 steel nail used as substitute for #5, and often cut off to replace #4, but only on the wings.*
B. *American ½-inch, No. 18 steel nail, used on wings and as needed as a substitute for "A."*
C. *American ¾-inch, No. 18 steel nail, used for attaching fuselage skin and in other areas of the fuselage.*
D. *American 1-inch, No. 18 steel nail, used on wings to replace #6, and on the fuselage for attaching skin panels in the upper engine bay area between #1 and #3 bulkheads.*

This before-restoration view of the underside of the top wing shows the cross wire and compression bar system. The top half of two ribs were completely missing and were later repaired by adding the new wood to the remaining portions of the original ribs. The front spar was broken just outboard of the compression tube between ribs two and three, right.

Temporary lines are attached to the landing-wire fitting at the lower right wing strut attachment point. On this right wing, pulleys of blue-purple anodized aluminum with brass bearings are for aileron control cables, while on the left, the pulley assembly was all magnesium. The steel compression bar shown here in the right wing was not installed in the left wing.

When the main structure of the top wing was completed, this special rack was built to handle the wing in nearly any position to facilitate adding the many other details. Note the ground wire threaded through the wing-tip ribs. This was soldered to compression bars and other metal parts.

Details of the left lower wing compression bar near the butt rib are shown in this view. Three steel bars for each lower wing were first incorporated in the D.III in April-May 1917 to aid in averting chronic wing failure. Based upon the original workmanship of these two lower wings, it was apparent that the right wing was built more hurriedly than the left.

This is a general view of the working area for the restoration of the Albatros. Richard Horigan, left, and Garry Cline, devote twenty-six months to complete this restoration project.

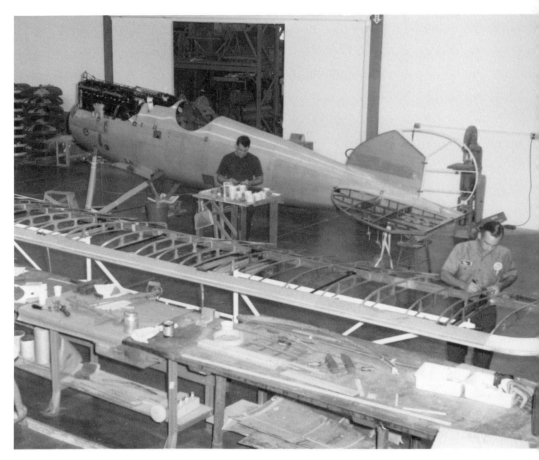

It was difficult to differentiate visually between the original aileron and the newly fabricated right aileron. The new tubing was thicker and therefore heavier.

The completed wings were varnished as in the original configuration; however, for this restoration, two coats of Polyurethane epoxy varnish were used. The original reddish tint remained in the wood of the lower left wing and was varnished over. The trailing edges were formed by a wire held in place with a metal clip over the end of the wing rib.

Shortly after starting the project, Cline discovered that the two lower wings were not a matched set. They appeared to have been made at the same factory, but at widely spaced times. The left, for instance, had two metal compression stiffeners between the main spar and the leading edge, while the right had three which is believed to have been the standard. The butt ribs were constructed differently on each side of the two lower wings. In addition, rib-strip lacing with black thread was used on one wing while white thread was used on the other wing. Most noticeable was the red tint varnish on the left wing, while the other was nearly clear. All this had little effect on the finished restoration, but it was interesting that no two of the three wing panels were of a set for this Albatros.

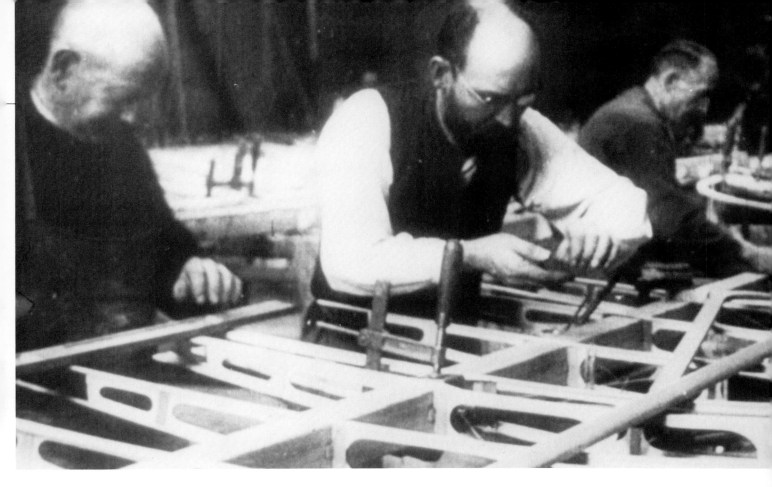

The top wing is assembled in the Albatros factory very much in the same fashion that the restoration was performed sixty years later. Approximately 150 Albatros fighters were manufactured per month during World War I.

Early German motion-picture film revealed a number of manufacturing details in the building of Albatros aircraft. In this view, a factory worker adds a cap strip to an Albatros wing rib. Other workers perform earlier stages of the assembly.

All metal fittings were cleaned, repaired, and painted in their original color. Internal fittings on the top wing were generally black, while the natural color fittings on the lower wings were coated with Water White for the purposes of this restoration. The entire wood structure had been stripped of its original varnish and given two coats of polyurethane epoxy varnish. The left wing retained its red tint.

When the three structures were completed, 2,226 man-hours had been devoted to their restoration. Included in this time was the fabrication of a new right aileron out of metal tubing using the left aileron as a pattern. Although the new tubing nearly matched the material originally used on the left aileron, the new structure is noticeably heavier since the tubing walls are thicker. Thin stock to match the sixty-year-old tubing could not be located.

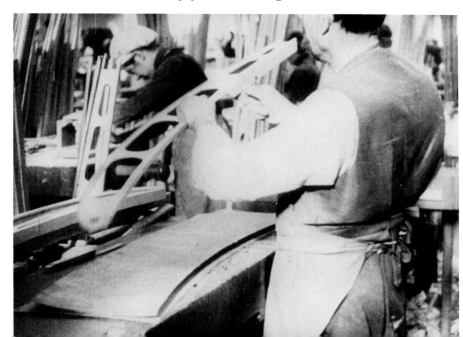

Lozenge Camouflage Fabric

A detail not normally encountered in restorations was the need to obtain fabric that was specially printed before it was affixed to the airframe. This was required on the museum's Albatros D.Va, for its date of manufacture in 1918 was after it had been decreed that all newly built German aircraft would have printed fabric. How this precolored fabric became adopted for use on German aircraft is a story all its own, but a brief background of this method of camouflage is worthy of note at this point.

Prior to the introduction of camouflage, the majority of German military aircraft simply had the unbleached linen fabric coated with clear dope. Over this was a final protective varnish, resulting in a "white" appearance which was often used to describe German aircraft in early Allied combat reports.

Women factory workers hastily tie the reinforcement tapes to the top wing of an Albatros. These early factory photos are frames copied from motion-picture film.

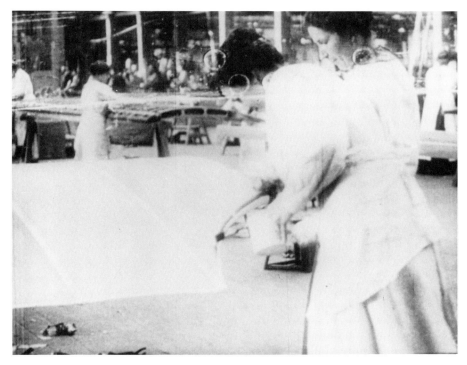

Many women were employed in the aircraft industry during World War I, and they did much of the extensive fabric work on these early airplanes. Shown here are two women applying dope to the Albatros trailing-edge tapes.

Camouflage was introduced during 1916 and the initial scheme had the aircraft finished on the upper and side surface in large irregular hand brush-painted patches of either green and reddish brown, or mauve and green. This was applied in a pattern similar to the "shadow shading" that was used on U.S. Air Force aircraft in Southeast Asia commencing about 1964. Greens varied from sage to dark olive, while mauve varied from lilac to indigo tinged with red. Undersurfaces were usually a pale sky blue, although yellow was quite often used.

In an effort to reduce the weight of the many colors and coats of paint applied to these machines, a preprinted fabric having a pattern of irregular polygons was introduced. This is commonly called the "lozenge camouflage pattern," though by definition this is incorrect as the figures are not four-sided of equal length in diamond shape as the word is defined.

There does not seem to be a definite date for this change except for a directive dated April 12, 1917, stating that all new aircraft would be covered with the printed colored fabric. Obviously, aircraft would not be stripped of painted fabric and re-covered with new printed material. It was a case of new aircraft replacing old or lost machines; therefore, the change was gradual during 1917 and for a time, airplanes with both types of camouflage were assigned within the same air units. The first mention of printed fabric was in a German order dated October 7, 1916, calling for the return of all cloth held by plane manufacturers for the necessary color printing process, or to be exchanged for printed fabric.

The Germans adopted several basic geometric designs for printed colored patterns. If they named or coded them, this nomenclature has been lost, but when a study was made by interested individuals as late as the 1950s, two designs were given the identifying names of "Knowlton" and "Canberra" patterns which relate geographically to where samples were studied and recorded. Free-lance researchers, among them being J.D. Hastings of Mount Vernon, New York, closely inspected and recorded the four-color pattern of the well-preserved Fokker D.VII in the Brome County Historical Society Museum at Knowlton, Quebec,—thus the name. Of equal interest was the Albatros D.Va in its original form at the Australian War Memorial Museum at Canberra, which has a five-color camouflage pattern. Although there are records of variations, such as a larger pattern used for bomber-type aircraft, the so-called "Knowlton" and "Canberra" patterns were the most prevalent of the lozenge camouflages.

Linen fabric manufactured in Europe for covering airplanes was prepared in bolt widths recorded as 50 inches and 54 inches. The camouflage pattern was identical for both widths, but for the 50-inch material, the outer 2 inches of the overall design was deleted. The printing was from selvage to selvage through the use of rollers suitably cut with the desired design. One roller was required for each color; four were needed for the Knowlton pattern, and five for the Canberra design. Each design had two sets of dye colors, a darker set for fabric to be used for top and side surfaces of the aircraft, and lighter colors for bottom surfaces. There is seemingly no correlation of color values between the two pattern designs.

To acquire fabric of this preprinted type for restoring the museum's Albatros was no simple matter. Its acquisition, however, was begun sometime before the decision was made to restore the Albatros. Museum curators knew that this special fabric would be needed in the future for several of its aircraft, and costs of production would not become any cheaper or easier with the passing of time.

This project would not only be an expensive undertaking, especially for the relatively small quantity needed, but would also require a great amount of effort to ensure accuracy. The involvement of more than one museum to share production costs would be a logical solution. This proposal was introduced at the annual meeting of international aircraft curators in 1974 at the Naval Aviation Museum in Pensacola. After those in attendance considered their needs, three museums joined in this project of acquiring the special printing of lozenge camouflage fabric. They were the National Air and Space Museum in Washington, D.C., the RAF Museum at Hendon, England, and the National Air Museum in Ottawa, Canada.

The Canadian museum had a Fokker D.VII in its collection which had sufficient original lozenge fabric from which to develop the geometric pattern. This arduous task was undertaken by Assistant Curator A.J. "Fred" Shortt, of that museum. His finished tracing of 50-inch wide, five-color material showed a repeat of the pattern after every third polygon, or about every 18 inches. His drawing overlay matched with other pieces of the remaining Canberra design fabric which confirmed its accuracy.

Determining the proper colors in this pattern was to be the next challenge. While examining the fabric of this Fokker, Robert Bradford, curator of aviation and space at the Canadian museum, quite unexpectedly discovered that the internal structural aileron members had been tightly wrapped with undoped lozenge-printed fabric, presumably to prevent these members from chafing the outer skin. Because of the tight wrapping, protection from sunlight and retardation of oxidation had been assured. Under a microscope, Bradford parted the fibers to expose their true colors and matched them to Munsell color samples for a permanent record.

Once this documentation was done, copies of these findings of the Canadian museum's staff were sent to the curators here and to the RAF Museum for their review and comments. All agreed with the results and were satisfied that production runs made to these specifications would suit their restoration requirements for accuracy.

German Lozenge Camouflage Pattern

Similar To "Canberra" Pattern
Researched From Fokker D.VII, 3659

Colors: R. W. Bradford, National Aeronautical Collection, Ottawa, Canada
Pattern: A. J. Shortt, " " " " "
Drawing: R. C. Mikesh, National Air and Space Museum, Washington, D.C., U.S.A.

Symbol	Upper Surface		Lower Surface	
	Color	Munsell Code	Color	Munsell Code
A	Purple	5P 3/4	Purple	5P 4/4
B	Ochre	2.5Y 5/4	Yellow	10YR 6/6
C	Green	7.5GY 4/4	Lilac	5RP 5/6
D	Blue	5PB 2/6	Blue	2.5PB 4/4
E	Blue-Green	7.5BG 3/4	Blue-Green	7.5BG 4/4

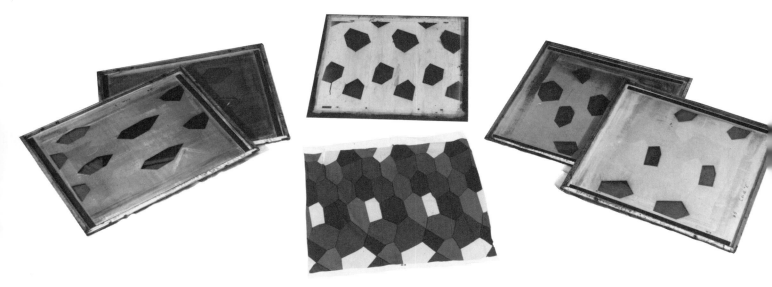

To obtain the lozenge camouflage patterned material, grade "A" cotton fabric was silk screened at a fabric-goods mill for this project. These are the five screens that were used, each with one repeat of the pattern which is 50 inches wide. A sample of the finished fabric is in the center.

The coordination for this project became the responsibility of this author. Much of the way had been cleared by Louis S. Casey, curator at the National Air and Space Museum, on an earlier and similar procurement. Greeff Fabrics, Inc., in Port Chester, New York, who had printed fabric for these museums in the past was asked again to help. As before, Albert Zellers, director of the Design Department, willingly undertook the task of having the cloth printed even though such a small project was unprofitable and very time-consuming. The total process had to be started from the very beginning. Since the original rollers were nonexistent, silk screens were prepared for the hand-printing process. Five colors required five screens. This became the most expensive part of the project, $900 just for the screens, but the cost was divided among the three museums.

Sample swatches were printed, reviewed for color accuracy by those involved at the three museums, and the go-ahead was given for production. To this point, the operation has been presented as though no problems were encountered, but there were many. Each museum supplied 200 yards of its own 60-inch Grade-A cotton fabric, but the material from each of the sources turned out to have differences in their ability to accept the dyes without color change, resulting in a blotchy effect due to the different fabric fillers. There were even problems and delays with passing the fabric across the Canadian-United States border and back again without undue customs charges. The results obtained with the material supplied by the National Air and Space Museum were very satisfactory, and the fabric was on hand by the time the restoration of the Albatros was started.

When it came time to cover the top wing of the aircraft, a decision had to be made as to the direction that the fabric pattern should run. For the Albatros D.Va, all known references describe the material as running span-wise with a 12-inch strip sewn at the rear to extend the fabric to the trailing edge between the aileron cutouts. This method is used on the Albatros at the Australian War Memorial Museum which had its original fabric. It is plausible that the only recorded descriptions for attaching Albatros fabric have been based on this one aircraft.

Of the twenty-three photographs of operational Albatros fighters that were clear enough to show the direction this fabric was laid, all showed it to be laid fore and aft. Obviously either method was correct, but since the original

While some Albatros are known to have had the cloth material attached to the wing from wing tip to wing tip, others laid the fabric chordwise which was the method used here. John Cusack (left) and Walter Roderick (right) join the top and bottom cotton covering with the prescribed baseball-type stitch.

fabric on the museum's Albatros wing ran fore and aft, even though this was lozenge-printed fabric, the new fabric was attached as in the original method. In support of this decision was a German directive which stated that aircraft were to be covered with the colored fabric in exactly the same way as with the earlier white fabric. The unprinted edges of the 60-inch material were trimmed off to achieve the 50-inch pattern.

There is no denying that the dope application on the restored Albatros used different dope and more coatings than when first manufactured in wartime 1918. This was of little consequence when considering the preservation benefits that were gained in using modern material and techniques. Butyrate dopes which are fire retardant were used on all the fabric surfaces.

The first coatings, though not used originally, were brushed-on fungicidal clear, followed by two coats of non-tautening dope. Surfaces were lightly sanded, followed by rib stitching over which were placed 25 mm-wide tapes with four pinks to the inch. One source states that these tapes were blue;

After the fabric was hand sewn around all the edges, it was dampened to remove all wrinkles. One coat of fungicidal clear dope was then brushed on, followed by several coats of non-tautening butyrate dope which was then lightly sanded. Karl Heinzel helped out with some of the 420 feet of hand rib stitching that followed.

however, salmon-pink colored tapes were found throughout the original lozenge covering on the lower wings, so the replacement tapes were made to match.

Three more coats of non-tautening butyrate dope were sprayed and again sanded, followed by two heavy coatings. The final coat was non-tautening clear-flat for, in a report prepared by the late Peter L. Gray of Great Britain, he quoted a German directive that states "the final coating would be matt lacquer obtainable from the firm of Cohn in Berlin-Neukolln."

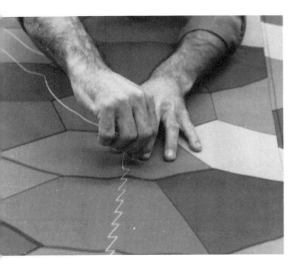

A curved needle was used to catch the reinforcement tape that was laced along each rib cap strip. Stitches are 30 mm apart. The dark border around the polygons is a deliberate overprint of the adjacent colors.

Across each row of stitches was doped a 25-mm tape that was pinkish in color. When the doping process was completed, the Iron Cross insignia was applied by hand brushing, but the edges were masked with tape.

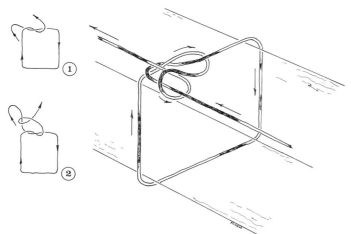

Rib-stitch knot for Albatros D.Va. This knot is first an overhand loop (1), secured by a half hitch (2). Loop ties are approximately 30 mm apart along the rib.

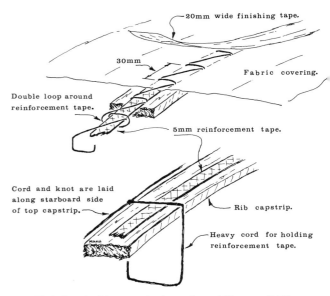

Fabric stitching method used on Albatros D.Va.

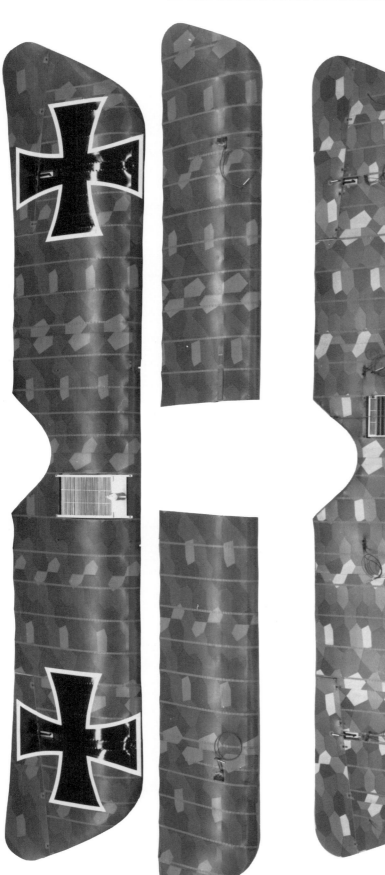
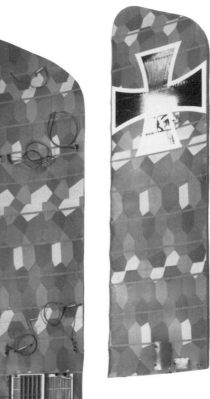

These record photographs show the finished wings, both upper and lower surfaces. The tone of colors are lighter for the bottom surfaces of the wing. Details of the radiator and its cooling louvers show well here.

White "Grade-A" cotton fabric without lozenge pattern was used for covering the tail surfaces since it would be painted in its final configuration. Richard Horigan trims the leading-edge lap, while the author-curator of the Albatros restoration project follows the work closely.

The stabilizer for the Albatros was of a very unusual design in that it had such a lengthy chord. Few replacement parts had to be made since damage was minimal. The structure was cleaned and nearly every joint had to be reglued. Some rib splints are in evidence here. Note the hole-punched plate for the four bolts that hold the tail-skid internal bracing wires.

Empennage

Restoring the tail presented a few problems that were not anticipated. To begin with, all that remained of the rudder was the forward hinge post. The remainder had been removed years before the airplane was taken from exhibit at the De Young Memorial Museum in San Francisco. Why someone had torn away the rudder behind this structure member is hard to explain, for it was far simpler to merely remove the hinge pins. Fortunately, drawings prepared with reference to the Albatros at Canberra had been acquired several years before and a new rudder was fabricated, beginning with the existing hinge post.

The wooden stabilizers were in as poor a condition as the wings. Nearly every member had to be reglued; however, a full disassembly of the structure was not necessary. Much of the cracked wood needed splices for repair. Two coats of dope-proof varnish completed the structures and made them ready for fabric covering.

The welded metal-tube elevator required many repairs. The trailing edge is teardrop-shape tubing. This part of the tail is also unusual since it is in one continuous piece as it is attached well behind the rudder and offered no interference to its movement.

A replacement rudder for the one broken off was fabricated out of steel tubing and welded to the original larger diameter tubing at the hinge. Details for this rudder were acquired from the War Memorial Museum in Canberra, Australia, which has the only other surviving Albatros D.Va. These empennage control surfaces were covered with Grade-A cotton fabric.

The metal structure of the elevator was in poor condition. It was rusty, bent, and broken in several places. After chemical processes were completed to remove rust from both the inside and outside of this tubing structure, routine methods of repair were made. When completed, it was painted, as it was originally, a light bluish green, Munsell code 10G 7/1.

Since these surfaces were originally covered with white linen fabric, aviation Grade-A cotton was used as a close substitute for this re-covering. To have been compatible with the wing covering, they would have had lozenge fabric; however, the plan called for these surfaces to be painted in the manner in which they were received. The application of fabric was the same as on the original, and the doping schedule followed that of the wings up to the seven coats of butyrate non-tautening dope.

Final Assembly

When all the components were restored, final assembly began. This was the phase that had been looked forward to for many long months. The main effort for this phase had already been accomplished several months earlier when the Albatros was assembled and before the wings and tail were covered with fabric. None of the original struts came to the museum with this airplane, nor were adequate drawings or rigging diagrams available. There was but one way to do this, according to Garry Cline, and that was to position and align all components in their proper location in relation to the fuselage, and make the struts to size.

Using the little dimensional information that was available, plus a few key dimensions and detailed photographs obtained from the Canberra Albatros, the parts were put in place much like a model builder would set up jigs to use in attaching the top wing to a biplane model. The fuselage with its lower wings in place was rigidly fixed in a horizontal position. Using an A-frame to hold the upper wing, it was meticulously aligned above the fuselage. Plumb lines were hung from many points to check alignment. Once all parts were in the correct location, temporary wing struts were fabricated from sections of electrical conduit tubing by having the ends of each section flattened and holes drilled for bolting into position. Cardboard templates confirmed proper angles. When all seemed to properly align, each strut assembly was fabricated—one at a time—in the form it was originally and put in place. What seemed unusual was that none of these struts had a method of adjustment, they all had fixed bolt holes or pin attachment points. Perhaps some trimming was ac-

The many details that appear along the side of the fuselage of the Albatros and its landing gear are shown well here. There is a fixed spreader bar which held the main landing gear V-struts. The axle is allowed to move up and down, restrained by bungee shock cords. Only the safety limit cables are shown here.

The landing-gear shock absorbing system was simply a 13-mm rubber bungee shock cord wrapped four times around a bobbin on the axle and the bottom of the landing gear V-strut. A loop of steel cable limited the travel of the axle.

Self-locking blocks of wood joined by one nail provided a mounting method for holding the wheel streamlining aluminum disc. Cut to fit snugly, these ingenious devices have no direction in which they can be displaced.

Outer wheel discs are shown here in place, while the inner cover is removed to show the method of attachment. The heads of 5-mm round-head bolts are on the face of the outer disc while nuts are used to hold the inner discs. The square section on the outer cover is the access door to the tire valve.

A small winglike fairing constructed of plywood went around the landing gear axle and the spreader bar. Four units like this one made up the structure. The top and bottom halves were hinged together at the leading edge and spring latched at the rear. Two of these were side by side along the axle.

Electrical conduit tubes were used as temporary struts with adjustable ends attached. A gusset plate was then attached to fix their angle. Note the 4-foot carpenter's level clamped below the wing spar which was one of several strategically attached to the airframe to maintain a constant check on alignment.

The top wing was then moved into place and rigidly suspended under an A-frame. Several days were required to precisely locate the wing into its proper location above the fuselage and to have it squarely aligned.

The lower wings were then put in place. These had fixed points on which they attached to the fuselage, but their alignment was still a tedious task. Carpenter levels, plumb bobs, and string lines were constantly checked.

Using detail photographs of actual Albatros wing struts and dimensions and angles obtained during the assembly of parts, reproduction steel struts were constructed. Since the design made no allowance for adjustment points, every dimension had to be exact at the time of its manufacture.

complished through the external bracing wires. All this rigging was a very time-consuming and difficult task, yet it was accomplished as accurately as the available information permitted. One questionable matter was the dihedral used on the bottom wings, for no reliable record of this angle could be found. Two degrees were used as best could be determined from drawings that had to be presumed to be accurate.

Structural wire bracing presented other problems. Originally these were of metric size, and this type of cable was not available in the United States, nor could it be located in Europe. In desperation, Garry discovered a standard cable in stock in the United States that contained a core very close to the original unbraided cable size needed. Unraveling this large cable to obtain only the core strand consumed a lot of cable, but for the sake of exactness, this was the solution that was pursued. Cables cut to the desired length were prepared with a woven tuck splice at each end securing them to turnbuckles and fittings. Some original cables came with the airplane which did help the assembly process to some degree, and a difference can be detected between the original and replacement cables, primarily by the number of wires in the strand and lay, but there are only slight differences from the original diameter. The original standing rigging (drag wires) are 1×38 (inner core of 19 wires twisted in one direction, covered by 19 wires twisted in the opposite

The old art of tuck splicing of steel cable had to be learned by both Garry Cline and Richard Horigan since twenty-three new cables had to be fabricated for the Albatros. The newly fabricated cabane struts are shown in place. In the background, Horigan reapplies the well-known but unidentified name of Stropp to the side of the fuselage.

Many replacement turnbuckles and fittings had to be made at the time of assemblying the Albatros. At left, Chief of Preservation and Restoration Ed Chalkley examines the newly machined turnbuckles while Walter Roderick, Shop Foreman, and Harvey Napier, master machinist discuss ways of adapting modern fabrication methods to duplicate early German parts.

Taking on the appearance of an airplane again, the Albatros D.Va has all its rigging in place. All its struts had to be fabricated since no originals came with the airplane. The difference in construction techniques of the upper and lower wings is apparent in this view.

With a wooden template made from the paper pattern, the "metal bending" process began. The cowling edge was established and a lip curled around it. After trimming the edge evenly, heat from a torch and a pneumatic hammer finished laying down the edge.

To produce the convex surface, the sheet aluminum was stretched across a form with an air hammer. There was no fast method of completing this process since every square inch had to be given personal and skillful attention to obtain a smoothly contoured surface.

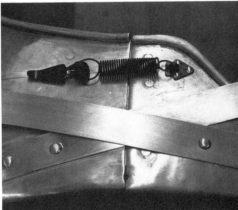

New engine cowls had to be fabricated for the Albatros and the Mercedes engine. Bill Stevens began by making heavy paper patterns of the various pieces. The spinner was put in place to provide the shape to which the contour was to conform.

This detail view at the top front of the engine cowl shows the spring clip that holds the two pieces together. For added support, two straps—riveted in place—cross, and come down either side to a latch clip.

The cowling nears final form as Bill Stevens adds the finishing adjustments. A wooden collar placed on the propeller hub provided a form to be matched by the cowling.

The aircraft serial number was cut out of masking tape and painted in heavily with a brush and black paint as was done originally. The curator of this aircraft restoration project, Robert Mikesh, watched as the permanent identification was once again applied.

Green and yellow Jasta 46 colors were painted over the serial number as was the case when the airplane was operational. Due to the heavy application of paint on the numbers, they are slightly raised and visible as a permanent identifier.

Recording the structural detail and restoration technique on film was the responsibility of Dale Hrabak, the museum's photographer. An attempt was made to photograph every detail for future study and technical reference.

The anomometer on the right wing strut for inflight airspeed reading completed the instrumentation. Graduations are in kilometers per hour times ten. In anticipation of this restoration several years earlier, this instrument was acquired from the National Technical Museum in Prague, Czechoslovakia, in exchange for an airspeed indicator to complete their Piper J-3 Cub.

direction), while the running rigging (flying wires) are 7 × 12 (7 strands consisting of 12 wires each). Replacement standing rigging became either 1 × 19 or 1 × 38, while running rigging is 7 × 19. In all, 13 cables are original to this airplane, and 23 are of new material.

Once all rigging was checked for proper alignment, the Albatros was disassembled so that the wings could be fabric covered.

Long before this stage, the landing gear had been restored and put in place. This phase was no easy task, for about all that was on hand were the main axle and two rusty landing-gear V-struts; both struts had their streamline tubing bent. Missing was the spreader bar to hold the struts in place while the axle floated on bungee shock cords. Using dimensions obtained from the Albatros in Canberra and checking against the length of the cross-tie cables, a spreader-bar assembly was reconstructed.

Even the wheels that came with the airplane were a mismatch. The rims were of the same size, but one hub had a babbit bearing while the other had brass bearings, and both had slightly different grease fittings. It is presumed that the wheel covers would have been of spun aluminum; not having this capability within the shop, these were made from flat .025 soft aluminum cut to become conical in shape and the seam was Heliarc welded. With a stroke of luck, one wheel-cover mounting block remained wedged between

The backside of the wing strut to which the anomometer is attached shows the markings of an Albatros D.Va, along with the serial of the aircraft. The "R" indicates this to be the right-hand strut which would assist factory or in-the-field assembly. Cabane struts are similarly marked.

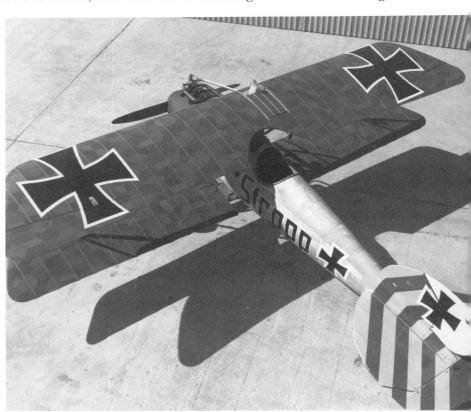

The techniques used in the restoration of this Albatros should extend its life expectancy indefinitely if maintained properly in a climate-controlled museum building as is expected. From a technological point of view for preserving the state-of-the-art of the time period of this airplane, the Albatros has been the most challenging restoration the museum has undertaken or plans to undertake for some time to come.

In a large gallery within the National Air and Space Museum, the Albatros fuselage was hoisted to the second-story balcony where it was then rolled into the World War I Gallery for assembly.

the spokes of one wheel which served as a pattern for the rest. Ten blocks per wheel provided support for a 4.5-mm bolt through these blocks to hold the aluminum wheel discs in place.

Tires for these wheels were obtained from Universal Tire Company from stock for classic car restorations; however, these do not fully satisfy the design that was used and the search continues for more accurate tires. Tires that were put on the airplane after its arrival in the United States were "Harburg-Wien" 760 × 100, but they had hardened with age and were unusable. Other sources show these tires to be "Harburg of Vienna," 700 × 100.

When the fabric covering was complete, the final assembly of the entire aircraft went quickly. Marking details had already been accomplished as each major component was finished. Therefore, when the components of the Albatros were assembled, the project came to a swift conclusion, almost anticlimatical. Details that remained incomplete at that time were the center-line fuselage stripe for field alignments and the few metal instructional placards to be attached to the main components. These details required additional research that could best be accomplished after the aircraft was assembled and were added to the airframe a few months later.

On a bright, sunny pre-spring day in 1979, the Albatros was rolled out of

Albatros identification placard. Five of these metal plates per aircraft were attached to the major airframe components.

In a setting similar to that often seen on the Western Front during World War I, the Albatros is in public view where it is admired by thousands of visitors daily. This Allied airfield setting depicts the Albatros as a captured airplane.

the restoration shop for the formal photographs that signal the end of a restoration project. Seeing the airplane complete in the daylight was a rewarding day for Garry Cline, Richard Horigan, and the many others of us who had a part in this project. As anticipated, this had been a challenging restoration, and a long one at that. Everyone knew, however, that a very worthwhile aircraft preservation had been accomplished that was truly representative of World War I history and technology. It was not long afterward that the airplane was moved to the World War I Gallery so that visitors to the National Air and Space Museum could see and admire this one of two surviving Albatros D.Va fighters, in the restored condition it rightfully deserves.

IV

Other Pertinent Data

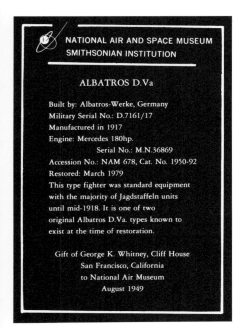

Each newly restored aircraft of the National Air and Space Museum has a mini-record placard of the type shown here. It is securely attached in the cockpit as a permanent record for that aircraft. Pictured here is the 5-inch-high metal plate containing the pertinent data about this Albatros D.Va.

CONDENSED WORK-PROGRESS LOG OF THE ALBATROS D.V A

1977

1. January 13 — Project began. Fuselage adapted to stand. Removed fuselage equipment and fittings. Cleaned inside fuselage. Markings traced. Began work on guns. Straightened landing-gear "V" struts. Started work on fuselage equipment, fittings, plumbing, etc. Engine disassembled for restoration. Repaired spinner and fabricated backing plate.

2. February — Worked on wheels, engine, guns fittings, and plumbing. Determined materials needed for total project. Listed parts requiring machine-shop assistance.

3. March — Finished guns, worked on plumbing, spinner, fuel and oil tanks. By mid-month, engine restoration was nearly completed. Wood supplies arrived and woodwork began on empennage and fuselage.

4. April — Fuselage woodwork on aft section was in progress. Worked on wheel covers and wheels, landing-gear struts and spreader tube.

5. May — Continued with fuselage woodwork, shock-cord bobbins, and fittings.

6. June — Fabricated pilot seat and rudder. Molds were started for forming plywood for aft fuselage-compound curved pieces.

7. July — Work included rudder, horizontal stabilizers, elevator, fuselage fittings, ailerons, and radiator. Fuselage woodworking continued.

8. August — Fuselage woodwork continued in empennage area. Control surfaces were finished along with radiator and its shutters. Work began on lower left wing.

9. September — Work continued on wing, and fuselage re-skinning. Cockpit coaming skin and major bulkhead repaired.

10. October — Worked on fuselage skin, miscellaneous wing fittings, and ammo boxes. October 26: Rich has 8 lb. boy!

11. November — Fuselage re-skinning continued. Lower left wing was completed, varnished, and ribs stitched. Began lower right wing.

12. December — Worked on fuselage skin, lower right wing, and fabricated ammo-belt collecting box.

	1978	
13.	January	Lower right wing completed and varnished. Fuselage skin complete in empennage area, along top to cockpit, and along belly. Began skinning right side of fuselage forward of tail. Worked on ammo boxes.
14.	February	Repaired landing gear, axle, and spinner cables. Continued with fuselage skin. Began top wing, and radiator pipes. Prop returned from Sensenich.
15.	March	Fuselage skin and top wing continued. Prepared compass and its bracket.
16.	April	Continued with fuselage re-skinning and top wing.
17.	May	Continued with fuselage re-skinning and top wing.
18.	June	Continued with fuselage re-skinning and top wing.
19.	July	Fuselage skin completed and varnished. Work continued with top wing. Installed landing gear struts.
20.	August	Engine was installed and most fittings and fuselage items installed.
21.	September	Horizontal stabilizer restoration completed and fabric covered along with rudder. Top wing work continued.
22.	October	Completed fabric covering of empennage surfaces. Top wing completed. Many smaller projects finished.
23.	November	Positioned wings to fuselage and began wing strut fabrication. Made running rigging cables. Rudders and elevators installed.
24.	December	Wing struts completed. Made standings rigging. Have turnbuckles and ends made up. Fuselage markings applied. Began fabric covering for wings and ailerons.
	1979	
25.	January	Fabric surfaces completed. Airframe assembled and details added.
26.	February	Concluding details added. Project completed.
27.	March 16	Formal outdoor photographs taken.

Reinforcing tape is placed along the side of the radiator opening in the top wing by John Cusack. Fabric colors of the lozenge camouflage are brighter on this lower surface of the wing than they are on the top surfaces.

The completed fuselage of the D.Va stands in readiness to receive its wings (foreground). The meaning of the name "Stropp," obviously applied by the German pilot remains a mystery, but the yellow and green stripes were used by Jasta 46.

The old fabric removed from the Albatros wings was retained in rolls of corrugated paper. Technicians applying the new fabric examine the old material in order to duplicate the original sewing and final detailing techniques.

Excellent detail of the radiator and its control linkage is revealed in this picture taken under the upper wing. Note the machine gun and its ammunition chute protruding above the plywood fuselage skin.

Left side of cockpit shows among other things the pokerlike handle which serves as the emergency throttle linkage. This is only engaged when needed to function in place of the throttle on the control column.

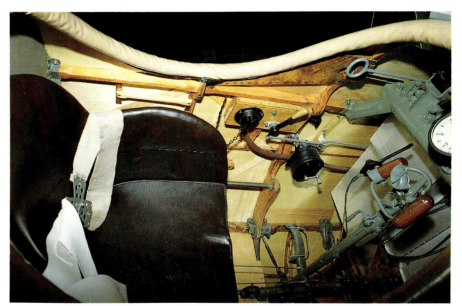

Looking forward in the cockpit of the Albatros, the most noticeable objects are the green machine-gun mount, and the aluminum-colored cartridge-belt container and ammunition cans. Fuel control panel is at the right.

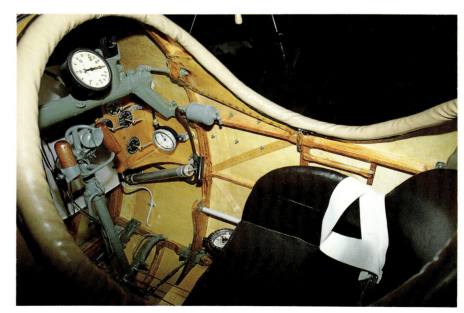

The difference in color of old wood on formers and stringers is evident when compared to the new plywood skin surface. The compass in front of the pilot's seat can be seen in this right-hand side view of the cockpit.

ALBATROS D.Va RESTORATION MAN-HOURS

	Fuselage	2,943
	Cockpit	374
	Engine	792
	Cowling	238
	Wings	2,226
	Empennage	404
	Spinner Mock-up	104
	Final Assembly	320
	Direct Restoration Total	7,401
	Chemical Cleaning	220
	Support Stands	80
	Programming and Planning	928
	(Missing-parts inventory, and outside acquisition, "How to do the Job" plan and preparation, etc.)	
	Total	8,629

ALBATROS D.Va SPECIFICATIONS

DIMENSIONS
- Wingspan, upper   9004 mm   (29'-6½")
-            lower   8730 mm   (28'-7¾")
- Length   7330 mm   (24'-0⅝")
- Height   2700 mm   (8'-10¼")

WEIGHTS
- Empty   680 kg   (1499.4 lb)
- Useful   235 kg   (518.2 lb)
- Total   915 kg   (2017.6 lb)

FUEL CAPACITY
- Main Tank   80 liters   (21.1 U.S. gal)
- Emg. (Aux) Tank   23 liters   (6.1 U.S. gal)
- Oil Tank   9 liters   (2.4 U.S. gal)

ARMAMENT: Two MG 08/15 (7.92 mm) machine guns with 1,000 rounds of ammunition each.

ALBATROS D.Va PERFORMANCE

SPEED: (1)

at 1000 meters (3,281')	171.5 km/h	(106.6 mph)
4000 meters (13,124')	154 km/h	(95.7 mph)
Maximum speed at 1500 rpm	172 km/h	(106.9 mph)

CLIMB: (2)

to 1000 meters (3,281')	4 min
2000 meters (6,562')	8 min 48 sec
3000 meters (9,843')	14 min 47 sec
4000 meters (13,124')	22 min 45 sec
5000 meters (16,405')	35 min

CEILING: 5800 meters (19,029')

ENDURANCE (3)

Maximum	2 hr 25 min at 1400 rpm
Combat	1 hr 30 min (10% fuel remaining in main tank, plus emergency fuel in reserve)

(1) Based on French S.T.Ae tests, March 14-16, 1918.
(2) Based on German climb tests, December 1917.
(3) Based on British tests showing 94.83 pints of fuel consumed per hour.

MERCEDES D.IIIA ENGINE SPECIFICATIONS
(Official German Specifications)

Ref: *Flugmotoren 1910-1918*, J.A. Gilles, Mittler 1971

Type	6 cylinders, in-line, over-compressed	
RPM	1450	
Bore	140 mm	(5.51 in)
Stroke	160 mm	(6.30 in)
Displacement	14.78 cu.cm	
Compression Ratio*	1: 4.64	
Weight (less fuel, water, oil)	268 kg	(590.8 lb)
Weight per hp	1.48 kg/hp	(3.26 lb)
Fuel Consumption at 1400 rpm*	220 gm/hp hr 54 liters/hr	(0.48 lb/hp-hr) (14.2 U.S. gal/hr)
Oil Consumption at 1400 rpm*	15 gm/hp hr 4.1 liters/hr	(0.03 lb/hp-hr) (4.38 U.S. gal/hr)
Piston Speed	7.7 m/sec	(25.26 ft/sec)
Maximum hp	180	
Carburetor	one dual Mercedes, twin jet	
Ignition	two ZH6 Model 14	
Starter Magneto	Bosch	
Identification plate on NASM engine	B.N.699.M.N70.hg GARANTIE.BIS.28.7.18 M.N.36869	

*Obtained from Ministry of Munitions Report on the 180-hp Mercedes Aero Engine, March 1918.

ALBATROS D.V AND D.Va PRODUCTION-BLOCK SERIAL NUMBERS
(Data provided by Peter M. Grosz)

Order Date	Quantity Ordered	Type Designation	Serial Numbers
April 1917	200	Alb. D.V	D.1000-1199/17
May 1917	400	Alb. D.V	D.1962-2361/17
July 1917	300	Alb. D.V	D.4403-4702/17
Total	900		
Aug. 1917	205	Alb. D.Va	D.5222-5426/17
Sept. 1917	250	Alb. D.Va	D.5600-5849/17
(Sept.-Oct. 1917)	600	Alb. D.Va(OAW)	D.6400-6999/17
Oct. 1917	550	Alb. D.Va	D.7000-7549/17
Total	1605		

AIRCRAFT SERVICING
(Translated from Daimler D.IIIa Mercedes Engine Operating Instruction Manual, circa 1917)

1. Fuel System

Filtering of fuel

While pouring fuel into the tank, a chamois skin must be used for filtering water and rust from the fuel. Due to water and condensation in fuel drums, this process must also be followed when pouring fuel from the supply drum into the servicing can, as well as from the servicing can into the aircraft fuel tank. Fuel systems operated by air pressure must have a 2-cm (¾ in.) air space at the top of the tank.

Closing of the filler necks

The cap screw on the filler necks of the fuel tanks must be tightened securely after servicing. Care must be taken that the seal ring is seated correctly to hold air pressure.

Fuel-line connections

Check cap screws on the 3-way cock valves for tightness. Ensure that all pipe fittings are secure.

Fuel gauge

Check that the cover on the fuel gauge is tight. (The tubing, through which gauge string [with its float at the end] travels, is connected to the main tank; a loose gauge cover would permit fuel to be pumped into the cockpit.)

Pressure check

By means of the hand pump, build up 0.25 atmospheres of pressure in the fuel tank. Check fuel and air lines as well as the regulator for possible leaks. System should maintain pressure indicating that there are no leaks.

2. ENGINE LUBRICATION

Oil servicing

For servicing the oil tank, the airplane must be placed in a level position. The use of a filter is recommended to catch foreign material. At or below 0° C oil must be heated before filling.

Points to be filled are:

(1) The oil reservoir tank.

(2) The lower part of the engine case through the vent pipe on the side of the oil pump on the engine. On the type-DIII engine, oil has to be added until it runs out the vent cock or until the oil level has reached the indicated height on the glass gauge. On the type-DIIIa engine, the oil level is replenished by a special pump to bring up the level in the wet sump system.

Lubricating the timing gears

After an extended period of inactivity, oil must be added to the cam shaft casing. To do this, remove the cam shaft housing covers over cylinders B and E. The 3-way cock valve in the oil pipe has to be open. [This 3-way valve is installed in a number of DIII-type engines.]

Oil the bearings of the valve rockers. Lightly coat the valve shafts and guides with oil.

Filling the grease cups

(*Engine*)

Fill the grease cup in the cockpit for the water pump. The stop on the spindle should not be in contact with the cover on the cap.

(*Airplane*)

1. Fill the grease cups for the tachometer drive.
2. Fill the grease cup on the hubs of the wheels.

Adding oil into the cylinders

After a long period of inactivity, one spoonful of mixture of ⅓ kerosene and ⅔ oil should be injected into each cylinder through the compression valves. [Do not use pure kerosene.]

Lubricating the magnetos and starter [booster magneto]

The magnetos have to be oiled once every 8 days, the starter [booster] every 14 days. Use animal oil or Vaseline oil.

3. HANDLING OF THE COOLING WATER

Water free of lime [soft water] is desired. Consequently, pure rainwater, boiled water, or water which has been allowed to settle [distilled water] is to be used. Water is to be poured through filters such as linen cloth. Do not allow dirt and foreign particles to enter the cooling system. The Daimler radiator has a filter installed in the filler tube.

Servicing the cooling system

The cooling system has to be filled to the top of the filler tube. Following this, 1 to 1¼ liters (1 quart) is to be drained from the system, so that there will be sufficient space to permit the water to expand as a result of heat expansion and to permit the water pump to operate properly.

Water cocks and vent cocks
When filling the system, all water cocks and vent cocks have to be opened initially. When it can be observed that a solid stream of water is exiting through the cocks, all cocks have to be closed, beginning with the lowest and continuing with the next higher cock.

Antifreeze
During cold weather, use hot water with glycerine or denatured alcohol added.

Testing the water pump during cold weather
To ensure that a portion of the system is not clogged or frozen, watch for air bubbles to rise in the radiator filler tube while the propeller is being turned manually. This will indicate that the water pump is working and that there is free water circulation. (As a precautionary measure, the ignition has to be switched off and the circular butterfly valves of the carburetor have to be fully opened—by moving throttle forward—before turning the propeller.)

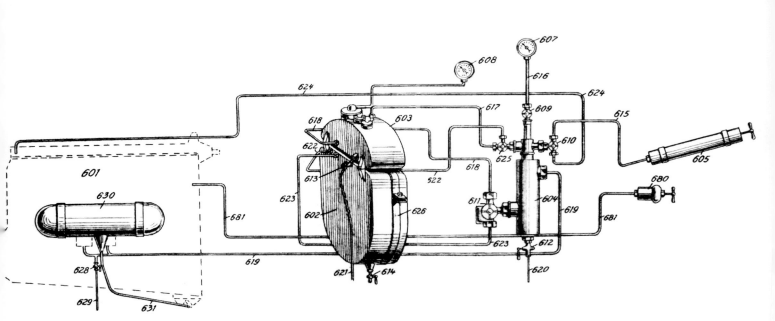

Albatros D.Va fuel system reproduced from aircraft parts catalog.

ALBATROS D.Va DRAWINGS

Due to the increasing interest by groups and individuals for making their own Albatros fighters, drawings have been prepared for presentation here to further document the technology of the Albatros and its time period. Of particular importance, it was discovered during the restoration of the museum's Albatros that wing-rib contours did not consistently follow the airfoil ordinates that were shown on earlier drawings. For this reason, samplings of specific ribs were traced during this restoration and recorded here for reference. These are located on page 115. Their location within the wing structure can be matched to the rib numbers shown on page 112.

By using measurements obtained from the Albatros D.Va at Canberra, Australia, along with other sources of technical data, Bob Waugh of South Australia, prepared dimensional drawings of that aircraft. These drawings constitute the most reliable structural information for the Albatros D.Va that has been located. During the restoration of the museum's Albatros, some differences—though minor—were noted, particularly in details and dimensions of the fuselage formers. This is understandable, however, when considering the manufacturing techniques that were used during the World War I time period. We are indebted to Bob Waugh for willingly allowing us to use these drawings for this publication. His eleven drawings appear on pages 104 through 114.

Supplementing these works, the author has prepared other graphic illustrations that appear throughout this book to record other details of lasting significance that pertain to the full-size aircraft, and which will also be of benefit to model aircraft builders wishing to re-create in miniature the "Stropp" Albatros D.Va.

The long-awaited day arrived on March 16, 1979, when the museum's completed Albatros D.Va was moved outdoors for picture taking. It appeared to be ready for take off and merely waiting for its pilot and attending ground crew to give chase to Allied SPADS and S.E.5s.

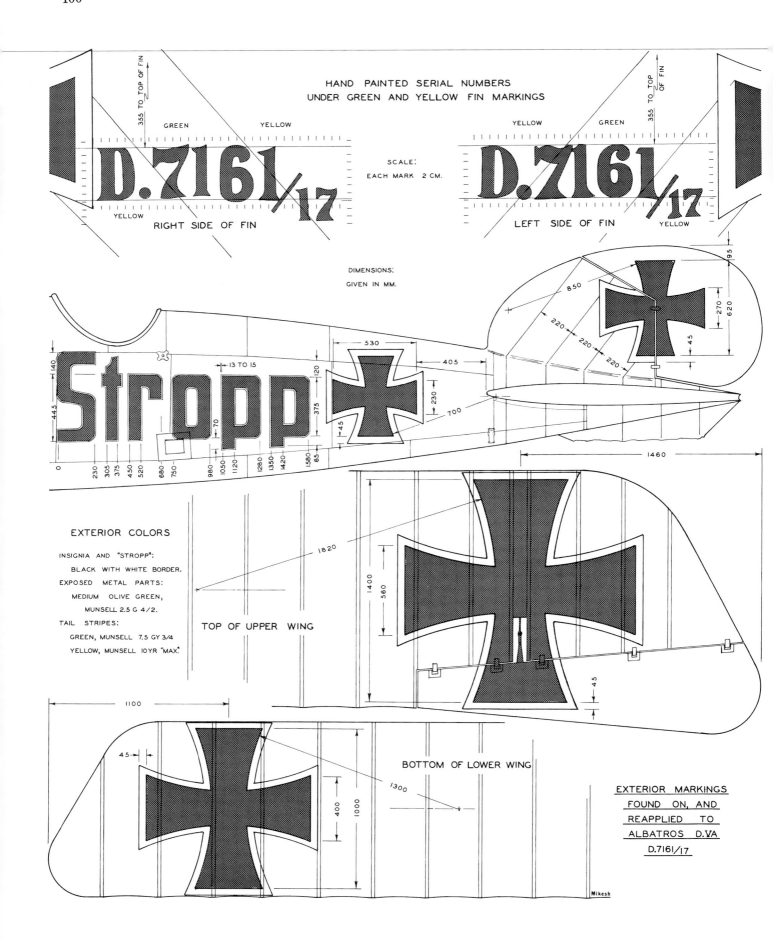

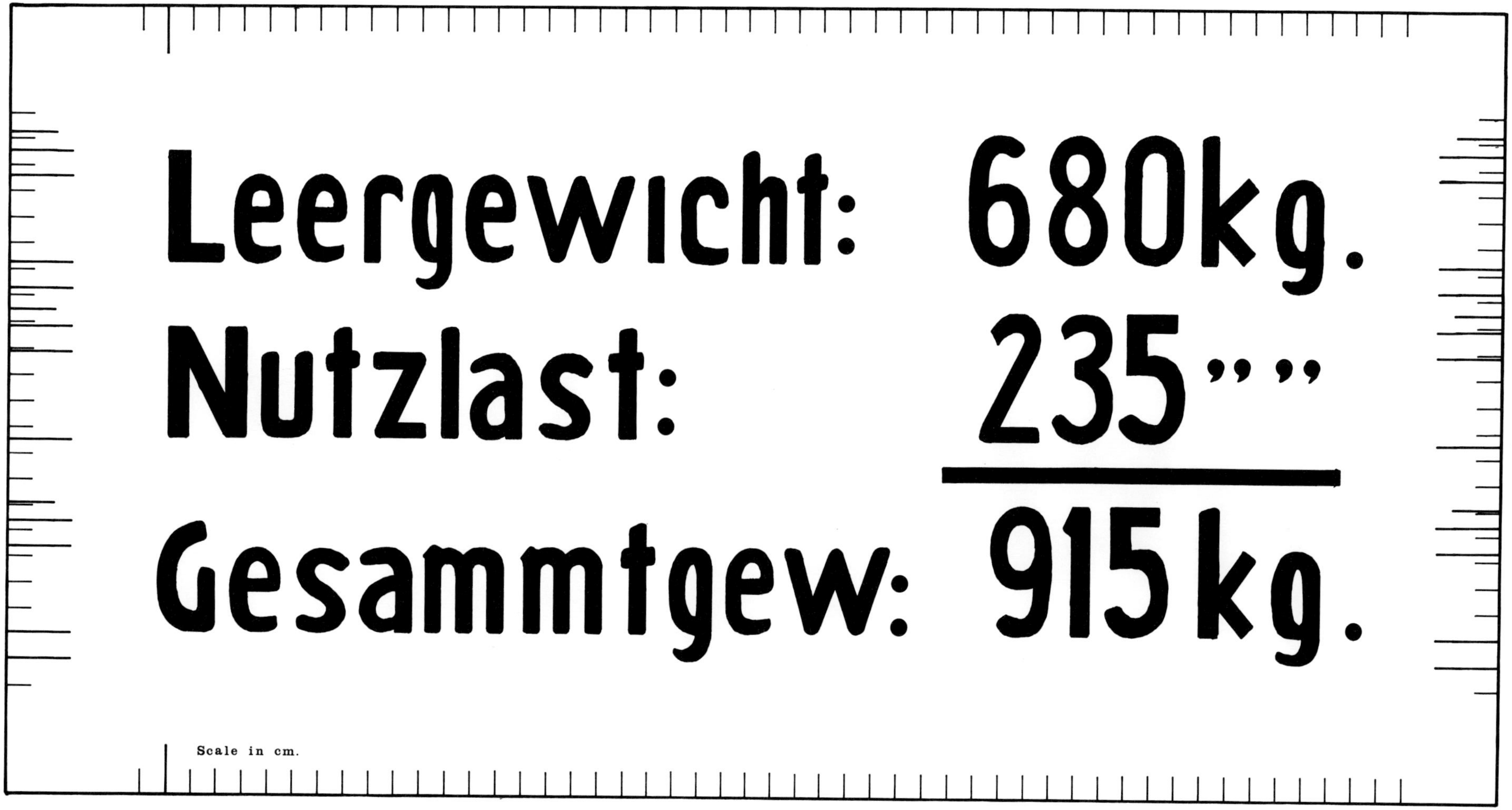

Leergewicht: 680 kg.
Nutzlast: 235 ,, ,,
Gesammtgew: 915 kg.

Scale in cm.

Albatros D.Va weight schedule, traced from original on D.7161/17 found at left side of fuselage.

1st run   Silver

2d run   Yellow

3d run   Red

4th run   Black

Silk-screen color separations for decals.

An extensive search was required to find an original Albatros logo with preserved colors that could be copied for this restoration. Dr. Martin O'Conner generously loaned his aged but original decal to the National Air and Space Museum so that color separation patterns could be drawn for making new decals. These color separations are presented here for others to use in silk screening additional logo decals should they be needed.

See page 90 for complete logo in color.

Full size

Propeller logo

1st run   White

2nd run   Black

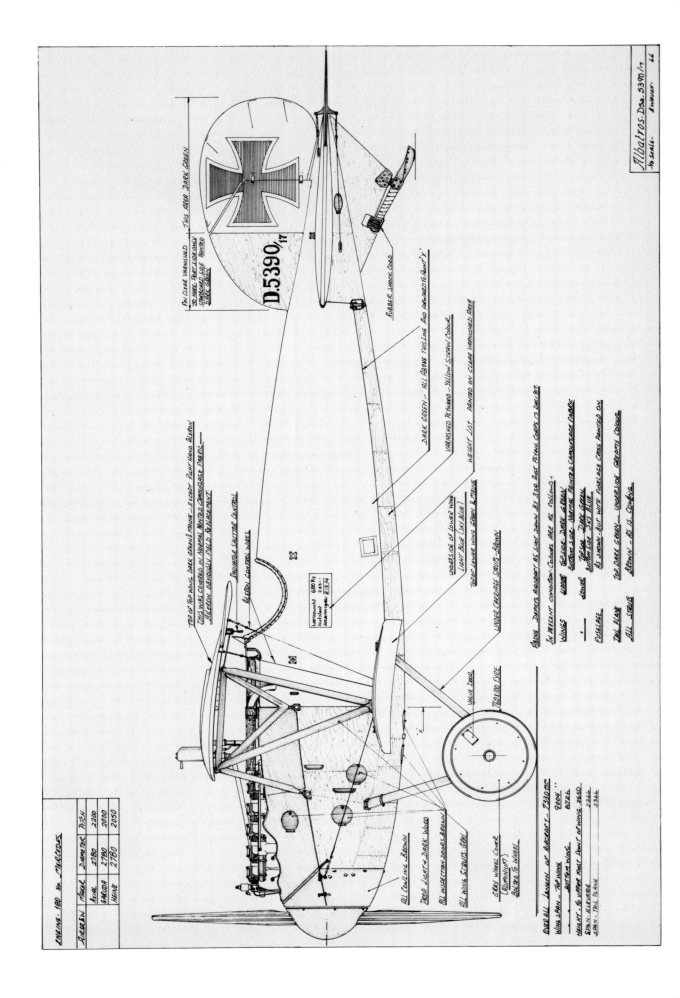

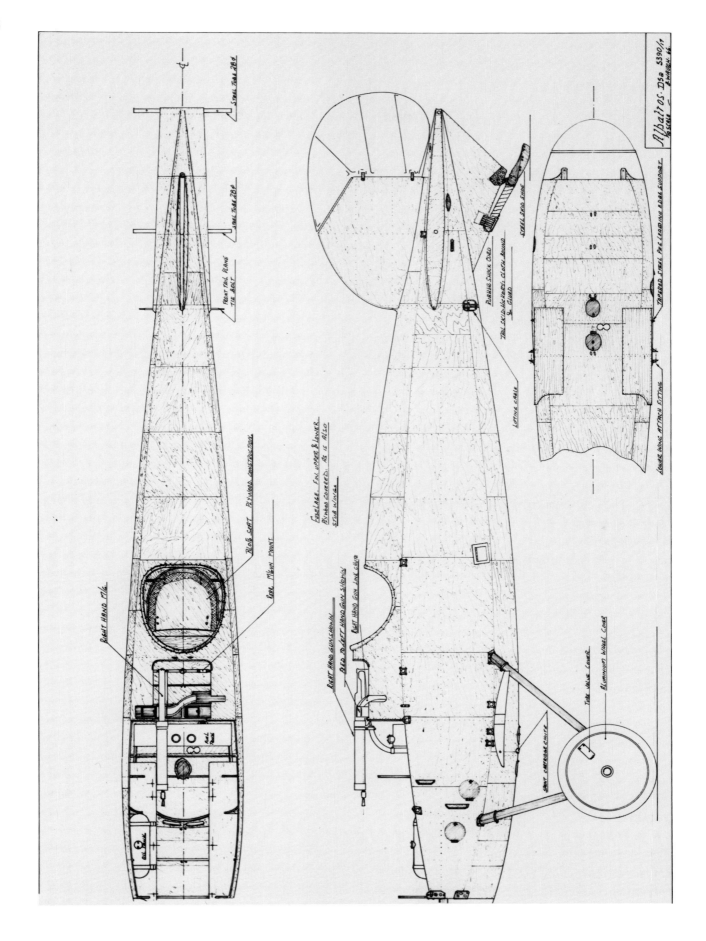

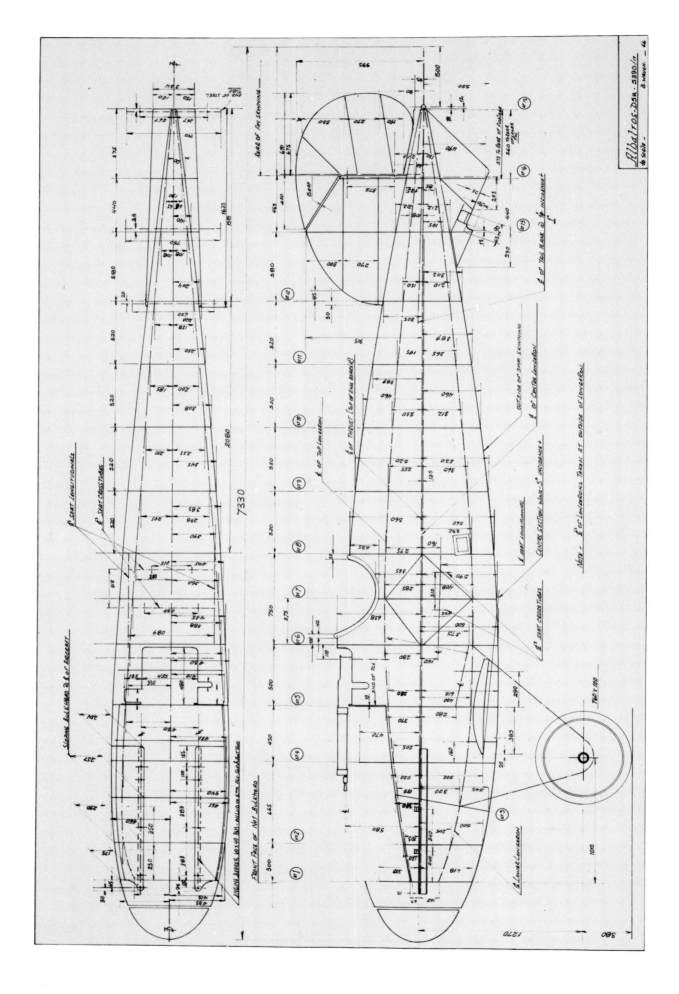

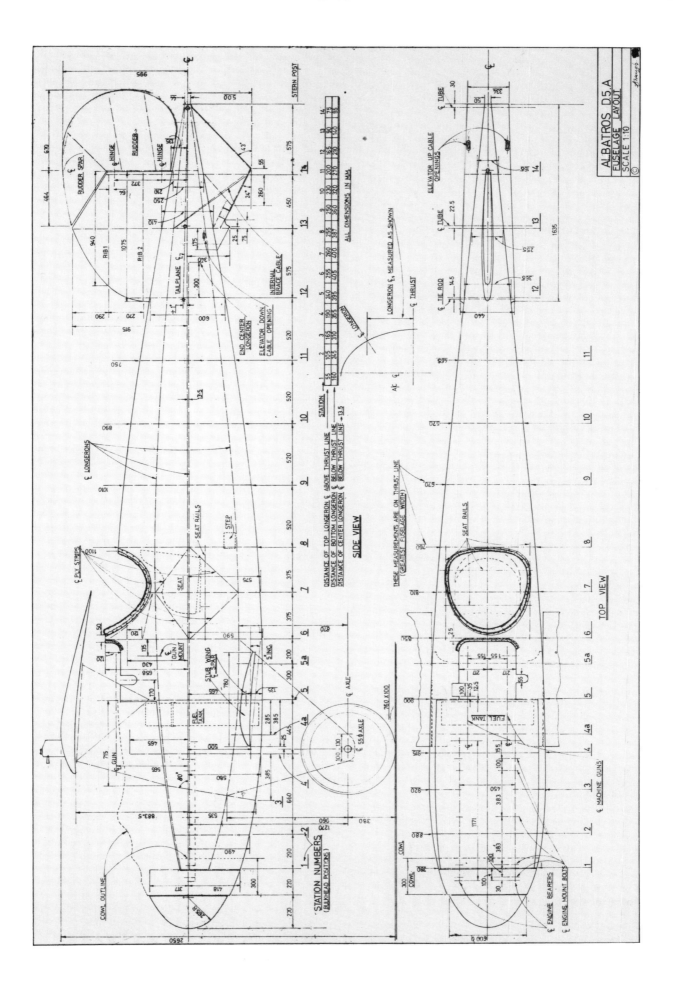

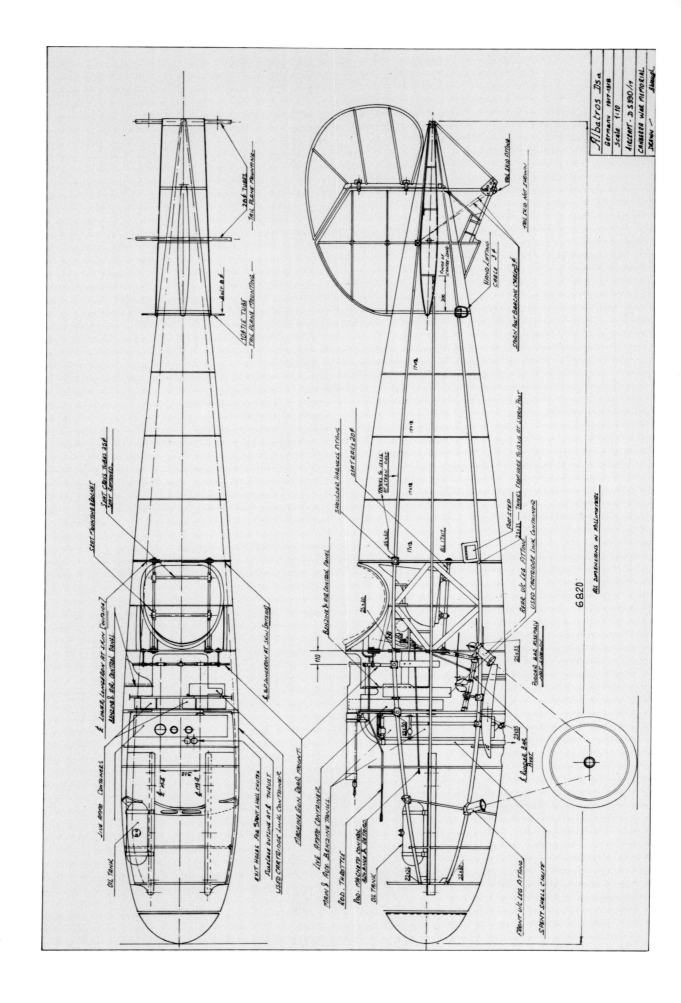

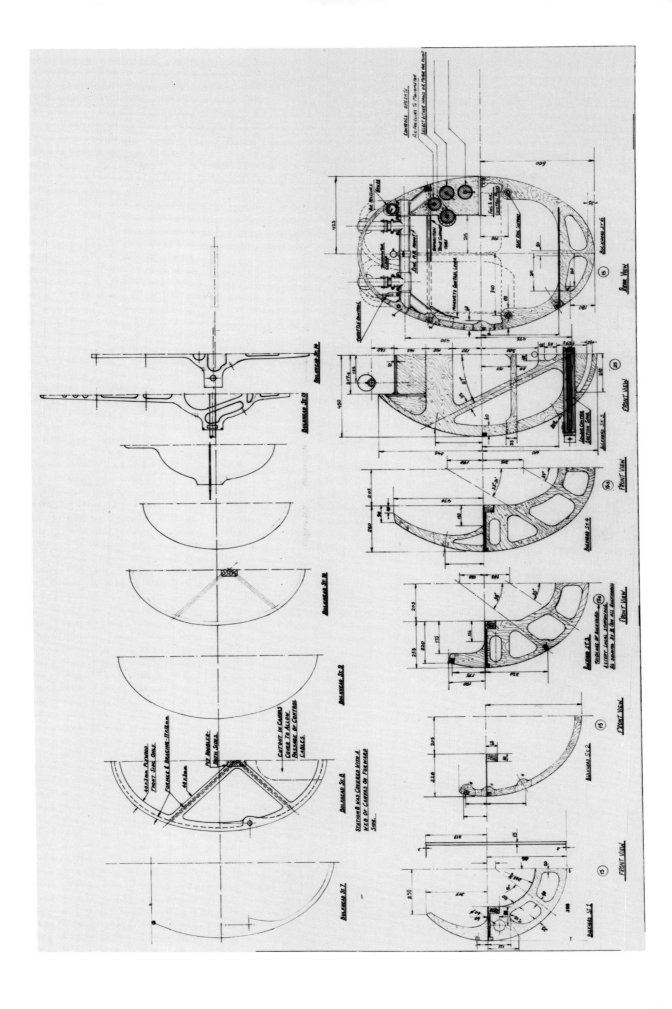

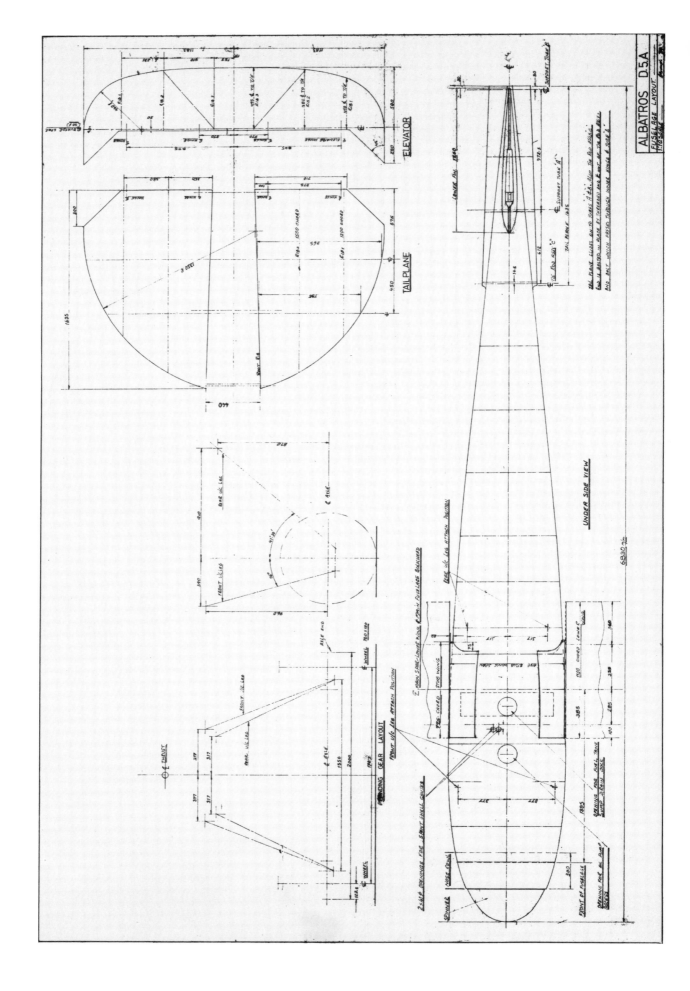

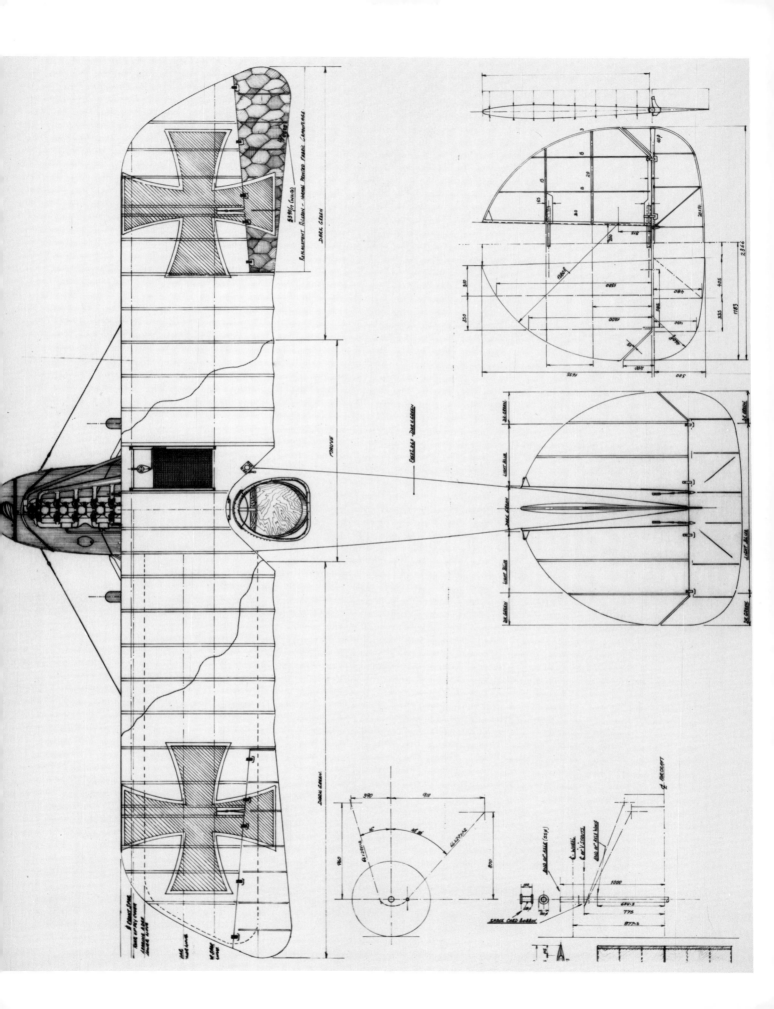

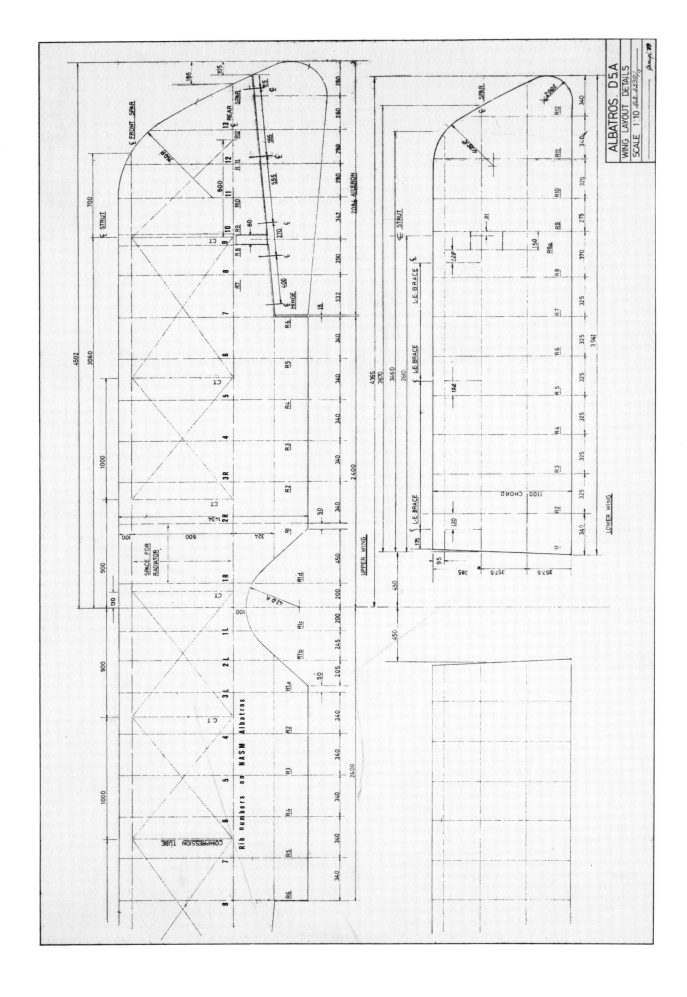

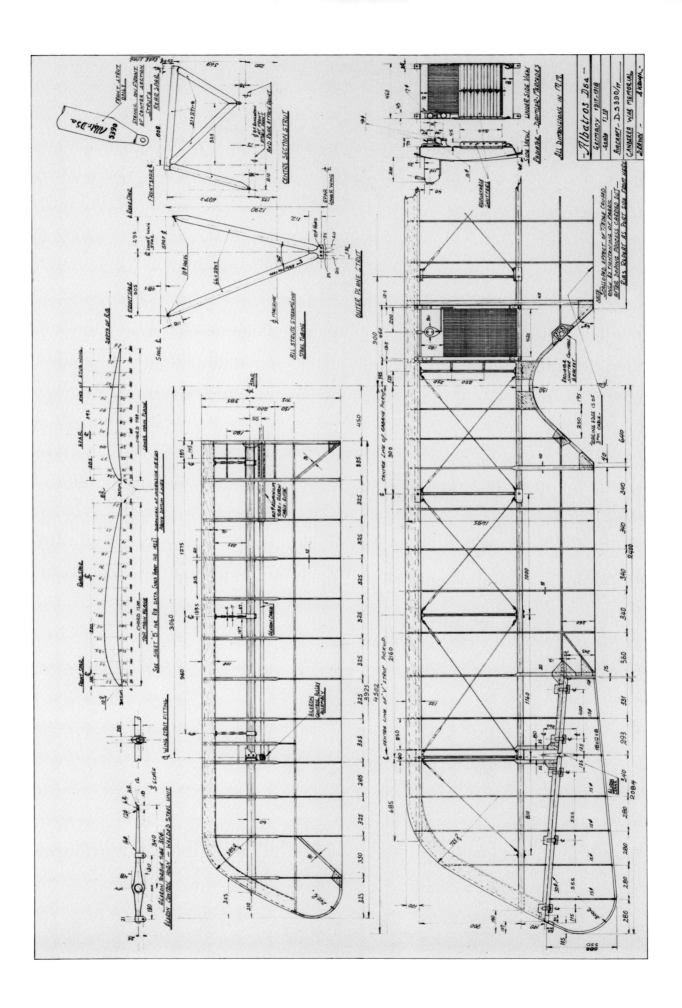

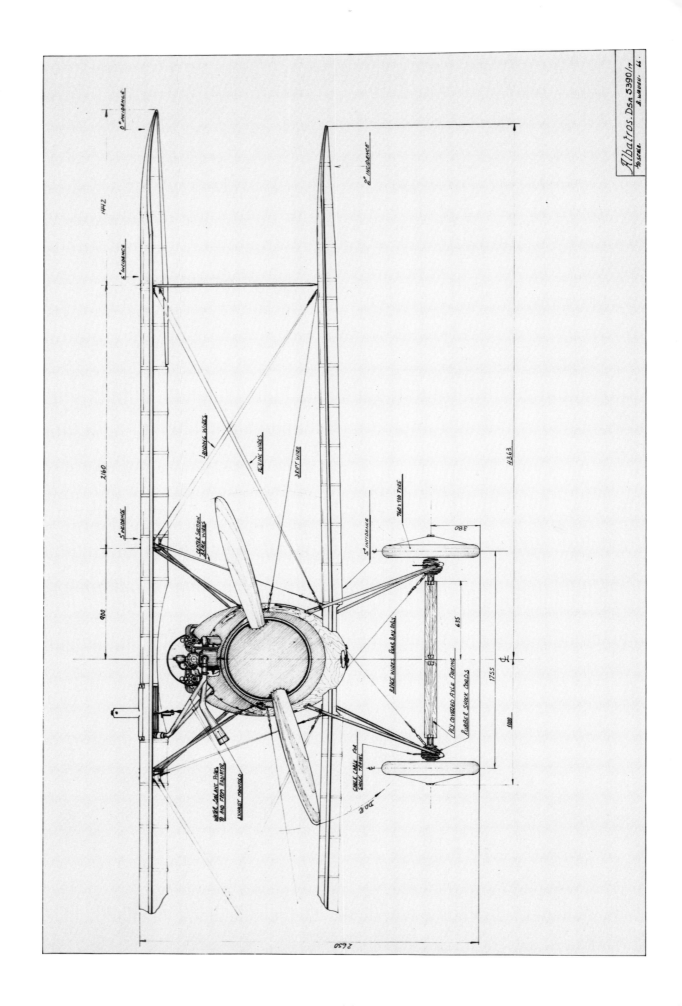

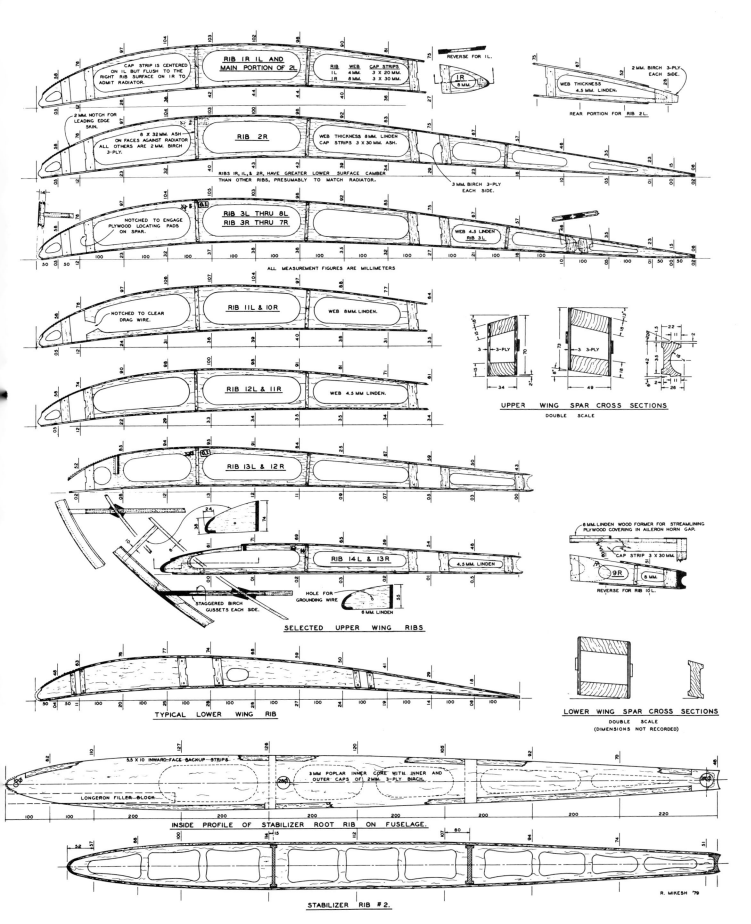

Albatros D.Va wing and stabilizer ribs.

ABOUT THE AUTHOR:

ROBERT C. MIKESH is curator of aircraft at the Smithsonian Institution's National Air and Space Museum. He is the author of the first book in this series, *Excalibur III: The Story of a P-51 Mustang*, which won for its category top honors in 1978 from the Aviation/Space Writers Association. Before joining the museum in 1970, he served as a pilot in the United States Air Force for twenty-one years, flying such types as Douglas B-26s, Martin B-57s, North American F-100Ds, and many others. With an avid interest in aviation since childhood, joining the staff of the National Air and Space Museum after Air Force retirement fulfilled a near lifetime ambition. His responsibilities include the accuracies in which museum aircraft, such as the Albatros, are restored. He has written several books and is a frequent contributor to aviation periodicals on a wide range of aviation subjects.